THE
FINANCIAL
BRIEFING

THE
FINANCIAL
BRIEFING

ANSWERS TO
LIFE'S MOST IMPORTANT
MONEY QUESTIONS

ERIC HUTCHINSON, CFP®

Published by Advantage, Charleston, South Carolina.

Member of Advantage Media Group.

ADVANTAGE is a registered trademark and the Advantage colophon is a trademark of Advantage Media Group, Inc.

Printed in the United States of America.

ISBN: 978-1-59932-659-7
LCCN: 2015957725

This publication is designed to provide accurate and authoritative information in regard to the subject matter covered. It is sold with the understanding that the publisher is not engaged in rendering legal, accounting, or other professional services. If legal advice or other expert assistance is required, the services of a competent professional person should be sought.

Special Note: Some portions of the information provided in this book were originally produced by the Financial Planning Association, the membership organization for the financial planning community, and are provided by Eric Hutchinson, CFP®, a member of the Financial Planning Association in Arkansas.

Advantage Media Group is proud to be a part of the Tree Neutral® program. Tree Neutral offsets the number of trees consumed in the production and printing of this book by taking proactive steps such as planting trees in direct proportion to the number of trees used to print books. To learn more about Tree Neutral, please visit **www.treeneutral.com.** To learn more about Advantage's commitment to being a responsible steward of the environment, please visit **www.advantagefamily.com/green**

Advantage Media Group is a publisher of business, self-improvement, and professional development books and online learning. We help entrepreneurs, business leaders, and professionals share their Stories, Passion, and Knowledge to help others Learn & Grow. Do you have a manuscript or book idea that you would like us to consider for publishing? Please visit **advantagefamily.com** or call **1.866.775.1696.**

TABLE OF CONTENTS

Dedication i

Acknowledgments. iii

Preface v

Introduction vii

FINANCE 101: LAYING THE FOUNDATION

I. Budgeting and Saving Basics

Ch. 1: How Do I Make a Personal Budget and Stick to It? 3

Ch. 2: How Do I Improve My Credit Score? 9

Ch. 3: How Do I Begin Saving and Investing? 15

Ch. 4: How Can I Grow My Savings?. 19

Ch. 5: How Can I Teach My Children Healthy Saving Habits? 23

Ch. 6: How Can I Help My Child or Grandchild
    Save for College? 27

II. Planning Basics

Ch. 7: How Do I Begin Developing a Personal Financial Plan?. 31

Ch. 8: What Should My Personal Financial Plan Include? 35

Ch. 9: How Do I Locate a Qualified Financial Planner? 39

Ch. 10: What Questions Should I Ask Before Selecting
    a Financial Planner?. 41

Ch. 11: How Often Should I Update My
    Personal Financial Plan?. 47

FINANCE 102: COMMON SCENARIO PLANNING

I. Planning for Unexpected Change

Ch. 12: Do I Have the Right Insurance Coverage? 51

Ch. 13: How Do I Respond in the Event of a Health Crisis? . . 57

Ch. 14: What about Disability and Life Insurance?. 61

Ch. 15: What Should I Know about Long-Term Care?. 67

Ch. 16: How Can I Help Older Relatives Articulate Their
Long-Term Care Wishes?. 75

II. Planning for Growth and Prosperity

Ch. 17: What's the Difference between Growth- and
Income-Oriented Investments? 85

Ch. 18: How Do I Narrow My Investment Options? 95

Ch. 19: What's a Municipal Bond, and How Do I
Choose One Wisely? 99

Ch. 20: How Do I Appropriately Allocate My Assets?. 103

Ch. 21: Should I Take an Active or Passive
Approach to Managing My Portfolio? 109

Ch. 22: What's My Real Rate of Return? 111

Ch. 23: How Can I Win with My Investments Over Time? . . 115

Ch. 24: What Types of Mutual Funds Should I Buy? 119

III. Planning for Taxes

Ch. 25: What Should I Do with the Money in My 401(k),
403(b), or Other Participant-Directed Account? 127

Ch. 26: Do I Need to Take Money out of My
Retirement Accounts after Seventy? 137

Ch. 27: Do I Have to Pay Taxes on Money I Withdraw
from an IRA Account?. 139

IV. Planning for the Next Generation

Ch. 28: Do I Need an Estate Plan? 145

Ch. 29: Should I Draft a Will, a Trust, or Both? 147

Ch. 30: What are the Benefits of Using Trusts to
      Distribute My Estate?........................ 149
Ch. 31: Do I Need a Living Will?..................... 153
Ch. 32: Who Should Manage My Affairs If I
      Become Incapacitated?...................... 155
Ch. 33: How Can I Make Sure Death Benefit Proceeds
      Aren't Taxed as Part of My Estate? 157
Ch. 34: How Can I Prevent Discord Among Family Members
      as My Estate is Distributed?................... 161
Ch. 35: What Documents Should I Prepare
      in Addition to My Estate Plan? 163
Ch. 36: How Often Should I Review My Estate Plan? 167

V. Planning for Retirement

Ch. 37: How Does Inflation Impact
      My Retirement Income?..................... 173
Ch. 38: Should I Assign Beneficiary Designations
      for My Retirement Accounts?.................. 175
Ch. 39: How Do I Transfer a Retirement Account?........ 179
Ch. 40: How Do I Get the Most from
      My Retirement Accounts? 183
Ch. 41: What Should I Know about the Default Investments
      in My 401(k) or 403(b) Plan? 191
Ch. 42: Should I Take Social Security Before "Normal"
      Retirement Age?........................... 195
Ch. 43: How Much Should I Withdraw from
      My Retirement Account?..................... 197
Ch. 44: How Should I Downsize an Empty Nest? 203

Afterword... 207
About the Author................................. 209

DEDICATION

For over thirty years, it has been my joy and privilege to work with clients and their families to help them manage their financial affairs and contribute in helping them meet their investment goals.

When I started out as a rookie trainee stockbroker at a large brokerage firm, I had no idea where my career path would take me. I only knew that I needed to know more about managing my own affairs, and I was convinced that there were others who needed help, too.

Along the way, as my own professional career evolved, it has taken me to some really wonderful places, blessed me with some amazing personal relationships, and enriched my life in so many ways. I am deeply grateful to my clients and their families for teaching me, sharing their lives with me, and allowing me to serve them over the course of their lifetimes and in some cases, beyond.

I am also profoundly grateful to my wife, Donna, for her patience, support, and unconditional love as I worked to build my career serving others with financial guidance. And last but not least, I'd like to thank my daughter Amy and late son Bryan for their encouragement, love, and understanding during the long journey to creating a successful financial services practice.

This book is dedicated to all of them.

Eric Hutchinson
Little Rock, Arkansas

ACKNOWLEDGMENTS

A special thanks to all of my clients, friends, and family who have patiently taught me so much over the years. This book is a distillation of real-life questions and answers, situations, and challenges faced by the clients I have served. From the bottom of my heart, thank you for allowing me to serve you in this way.

Jim, your friendship, wisdom, gentle guidance, love, and support have been invaluable. Pete and Betty, thank you for your insights, thoughtful suggestions, and loyalty over the years. You are missed. Pat, your sincere dedication to truly serving your clients was an inspiration to me and served as a model that shaped my career. Earl, thank you for your continuing questions that kept me on my toes and prompted greater learning to serve you and others more fully. David, your persistent yet good-natured ribbing kept me focused and on track. Don, your friendship and loyalty are priceless and inspiring and have sustained me. Charlie, your quiet strength, exemplary leadership, and commitment to your employees and customers have been a beacon of light in a sometimes all too bottom-line-oriented business world. Jim C., your infectious enthusiasm for life has always been a breath of fresh air to lighten my day. Rodney, your inquisitive, probing questions prompted me to dig even deeper to serve you and others even better. Jim A., thank you for providing an opportunity to share an experience of the real value of thoughtful financial planning. Judy, thank you for kindness, love, and understanding of what value there is in financial peace of mind.

Thank you to those professionals, mentors, and consultants with whom I have had the privilege to work. Garland, Don, Clyde, Leo, Dan, and Roby—thank you for your part in shaping my career. Your spirit, wisdom, and insights have been so important and valuable to me. Rose, thank you for your support, loyalty, and dedication to serving the best interests of our clients.

A special thank you to Paul, the man who is really responsible for planting the seed that grew into an amazing and rewarding career. Without his suggestions and encouragement, I might have pursued an entirely different path.

Finally, to my dear friend Greg, a bishop in the Episcopal Church, who recognized the value of laypeople bringing God's love to the community and serving them through their chosen profession. I will always cherish the memory of the laying on of his hands as he ordained me as a lay minister of financial services. I hope that I have been a good steward of that ordination and brought the love of God to my work helping my clients manage their financial lives.

PREFACE

Much of this book is a collection of the most commonly asked questions from clients over the course of my career and the answers that followed. Some are questions that surface at various stages of life, so not all of them may be relevant to you at your current stage of life. I suggest reading this book all the way through, as it will give you a broad overview of a great deal of the issues that most of us face over the course of our lives. Then, use the book like a reference resource to return to again and again as new situations present themselves in your life.

Share the book with friends and family when they articulate an interest about a particular topic covered in the book. Many give a copy of the book to adult children as a helpful resource to build a solid foundation for their financial lives.

For most, seeking help from a caring, competent financial professional that you feel you can trust may be well worth the time and money invested. Today's financial world has become an amazing, globally interconnected place that is often far too complex to go at it alone as a "do-it-yourselfer." A trusted financial advisor may be invaluable in the quest for complete financial peace of mind.

I wish you the best of success in managing your financial life so that your dreams come true.

INTRODUCTION

This is a book of distilled wisdom. Every person who has honored me with the privilege of serving them has been my teacher. They have allowed me into their inner circle, trusting me with many intimate details of their financial lives. They have made me feel as a trusted friend, allowing me to live vicariously through them as I learned more about how to serve them and others.

When an investment for a client didn't turn out as we had planned, I learned more about what to look for, what to avoid, and what I could do better in the future. When I saw my clients experience the loss of a spouse or other family member, or maybe a long-time friend, I learned more about empathy and sympathy and how to manage the grieving process. When my wife and I lost our son in an automobile accident, I learned first-hand about dealing with loss. While the loss of our son was an incredibly difficult and painful loss for my family, I grew not only as a husband and a man but also as a financial planner and advisor as a result.

This book is called *The Financial Briefing: Answers to Life's Most Important Money Questions* because—well, financial matters are complex, and people generally have a lot of important questions about how they should spend, save, and invest their money. To further complicate matters, life often throws curve balls, which can leave us face-to-face with financial questions we never thought we'd have to ask. When something disruptive happens, I know I can either be defeated by it, or I can learn from it. If I choose defeat, I lose everything. But if I choose to learn from all that life offers, good and bad, I can grow and even thrive.

When my clients faced big, life-changing decisions, I learned what issues were really important and what would evolve over time. Business triumphs, illness, tragic unexpected death, joyful celebration of a new grandchild, the vacation trip of a lifetime, a new business venture—I have lived and learned so much from my clients. In so many ways, I am grateful and honored to have been allowed to be part of their lives.

Out of all that experience, I am convinced that peace of mind regarding financial affairs is achievable. I have seen it many, many times. Even from disorganized, modest beginnings, a transformative change is possible. You really can eventually reign in all the disconnected pieces and get to a place of peace. It is not too late. Even if your life seems to be a bit of a mess right now, it is possible to turn things around. I know. It has happened to me.

All of us dream about how we would like our lives to be. Dreaming about our future, dreaming about a better tomorrow— these are part of being human. Life happens, and when it does, it is sometimes messy. From my experience, making dreams come true is much more likely if you have given some thought about tomorrow and developed a plan to achieve what is important to you.

Most people I have worked with wanted really basic things, human things. I have never had a client tell me they wanted to be rich or powerful—but I have had many tell me that they never want to be poor. Most tell me that they want to feel a sense of security, a sense of comfort, and a sense of peace of mind about financial matters. They want to have enough to live their life on their terms: enough to buy the things they want to buy, go the places they want to go, support the causes they believe in, and help their children and grandchildren get off to a good start. In short, they want to have financial peace of mind, even when life happens.

I am a positive person because I know from personal experience and close-range observation of many families over the past thirty years that the following statements are true:

- Dreams *can* come true.
- A feeling of security is possible.
- A sense of comfort is possible.
- Freedom from worry about money is possible.
- Financial peace of mind is possible.

The rest of this book captures some of the ways you may make these positive things happen in your life (and the online videos at www.thefinancialbriefing.com explain even more). The comments, stories, and tips in this book are the results of my three decades of working as a financial services professional. The topics I will cover here have been the most common issues that surfaced through the course of my career. I have kept track of some common scenarios and filed them away because I felt that they would be helpful to others someday.

I would like to start with a hypothetical story of Fred. *(Note: stories are purely hypothetical for illustrative purposes only.)* I think you'll see why it is a great way to start talking about the way a good plan can make a huge difference.

Why Planning Matters: Is it dangerous *not* to know what you don't know?

Maybe it is not dangerous, but it certainly can be costly.

Fred was a very successful forty-two-year-old executive with a large holding company involved in a variety of business enterprises. He ran several of the holding company's portfolio companies and was responsible for hundreds of millions of dollars in revenues to the firm. But at forty-two, he realized that he might not be on track to achieve his personal short- and long-term financial goals. After seeking help from friends and old college buddies who had gone into the investment or insurance business, he began to feel he was not getting the kind of guidance he really needed. Ultimately, he called a financial advisor for help.

After much conversation—and gradually including his wife in the dialogue—Fred agreed to start work on developing a financial plan for both his wife and himself. When the plan was finished, the financial advisor presented it to them, laying out the steps and stages it would take to get them on track to achieve their goals. One by one each step was implemented, following the plan as closely as possible. Toward the end of the first year of working together, Fred and his wife were clearly on track to achieving many of their short-term and even some long-term goals.

Reflecting on the progress they had made, Fred commented that in his role as an executive responsible for several companies, he knew every detail about the operations of every company in his area of responsibility. He knew every number on each company's financial statements and knew the impact of even minor changes in operations. Until now, he might not have been able to say the same about the business of life. Now armed with similar knowledge about his personal financial affairs, he felt empowered and confident about the future. He was proud of the progress he had made toward his goals and felt well on his way to achieving complete peace of mind about personal financial matters.

Fred reflected on how much he had learned and how much he had clearly been missing. He lamented that if he had this knowledge a decade sooner, he could have already achieved many of his dreams and goals. He said it was "bad enough not to know, but to not know what you don't know is downright dangerous."

FINANCE 101:
Laying the Foundation

I: BUDGETING AND SAVING BASICS

What you don't know about your money can weigh heavy on your brain. Free yourself from worry by starting with the basics. Once you know how to think about money, it will be a lot easier to understand the things you can do with money, so let's start there. I will add some useful tools for you to consider, but we'll begin with the most basic financial plan there is: a personal budget.

CHAPTER 1

HOW DO I MAKE A PERSONAL BUDGET AND STICK TO IT?

If you've been meaning to create a personal budget, but haven't gotten around to it, these reasons for doing so might be just what you need to get motivated:

You'll live longer and happier. Most doctors will tell you that stress can be a killer. Being in control of your finances reduces stress. Stress can make people eat more—and spend more—which affects both their financial and physical health.

You'll know what is important and what is not. Having a spending plan in place means you will have already prioritized the key activities, expenditures, and projects you will need to make for the year and the money you will need to afford them.

You'll be a better human being. Spending less time worrying about money means you will have more time to think about the people in your life.

Making a budget is a great way to understand your finances while saving your life and becoming a better person. And it's free!

Let's refine this very good idea a bit. Here are six effective methods that will help you build a better budget—and stick to the budget you build.

1. Track every dollar you spend.

Whether you do it with a pen and a notebook or a computer program, make a concerted effort to track your everyday spending. Physicians say overweight people should track every morsel of food they eat. With money, it is the same thing. Knowing where every penny goes makes it easier to spot where certain pennies can be saved or invested.

2. Prioritize your spending.

When it comes to spending, there are needs and then there are *wants*. It is important to know the difference between them. Get a big desk calendar (or an electronic calendar that allows space for lots of notes to yourself). Every day, make two columns and write down the items for which you *need* to spend and those for which you *want* to spend.

What are needs? You know what they are because life would be very difficult (if impossible) without them: food, monthly rent or mortgage payments, tuition, automobile payments, electricity, water, heat, insurance payments, retirement savings, income and property taxes, and credit card payments.

What are wants? It is not as simple to make this list because nobody wants to admit they don't actually *need* certain things: vacations, a poolside bar or other non-essential home improvement projects, restaurant meals, and so on. However, if you are honest with yourself, you should be able to intelligently discern what a need is and what a want is.

Once you've recorded your daily list of wants and needs, compare the total expenditures to your total income.

What will this crowded calendar tell you?

You will be able to see that, by addressing your needs first—attacking debt, making certain sacrifices, and spending and saving smarter—you can balance your finances and eventually be able to afford more of the wants on your list.

3. Review your budget each month.

There has to be a living, breathing side to budgeting that accommodates change. Near the end of each month, make a list of the specific needs and wants you'll face next month, total the cost of the needs, and figure out how much money you'll have for wants after your needs are met. For example, if your car needs a necessary repair, that is certainly going to boost the "needs" side of the page.

If there is a one-time event, like paying off a particular credit card or a once-a-year bonus, then it is important to decide whether it is time for something you want—or time to throw more into the things you need. Maybe, if you are thoughtful, you will be able to do some of both.

4. Identify and plan for long-term goals.

One of your biggest needs is to think about the things you really want to do with your life and what those things will cost. Putting goals in writing gives them a formality and a starting point for the planning you must do. If these goals require saving, make sure you put those savings dates on the financial calendar you made.

5. Build failure and recovery into the plan.

How many diets have evaporated with the words, "I blew it," and then it's back to the old habits that got us in trouble in the first place? The fact is, with food or money (or love), everyone goes off course at times.

We're all human. We all make mistakes. The mistakes, however, are less important than being able to learn from them and fix them. So make sure you have a plan for corrective action.

If you're about to make an impulse purchase, implement a three-day spending rule. That means you should give yourself three days to check your budget and think through the purchase before you make it. If you can minimize the damage that comes from impulse spending, your progress will continue.

If you get off course, recognize the fact, deal with it appropriately, and then move quickly to get back on course. With consistent effort and paying close attention to the details, you can develop a sensible budget and stick to it. You will be in control of your financial life and you will feel more confident about your financial future. A good budget is something you can live with. Wrap it around your life and take comfort in it. With a budget, your financial life is more under control.

6. Don't be afraid to ask for help.

Do you know where you need to be financially and how you will get there? A qualified financial planner can ask the right questions, help you provide useful answers, and guide you as you work to develop a customized plan to reach your financial goals. A trusted advisor can help you think through major financial decisions so you keep yourself on track. In other words, a trusted advisor can help you make smart choices about your money.

CHAPTER 2

HOW DO I IMPROVE MY CREDIT SCORE?

Once you're budgeting your money wisely, you'll want to also consider your credit score, which can tell you a lot about your financial standing and how risky potential lenders may perceive you.

If you're planning to buy a home or a car these days, the process may be a lot tougher without an excellent credit score and a significant down payment. So that means you're going to have to work harder—and possibly wait a little longer—to make those key purchases. It is particularly important to make sure there are no skeletons in your credit closet.

High levels of debt, combined with a global credit crunch, have tightened up lending to all but the best customers—and even some very credit-worthy customers are having trouble too. If you have extraordinarily high debt levels, a record of late payments, or very little money to put down on that home or car, then you need to do some advance planning before you contact any lenders.

Here are six things you should incorporate into your planning so you will be ready to use your credit wisely when then time comes:

1. Get some advice.

You might be focused on paying down debt or saving up for your down payment on that new home or car, but credit is only one part of your lifetime financial picture. It might be a good idea to talk with a qualified financial professional to learn how to best use credit. It is always good to determine what your limits should be and to understand the rules of the credit game.

2. Pay down the balances you have.

The Fair Isaac Corporation, the company that created the FICO score, has adjusted the way it computes its credit scores. One of the top changes is a greater negative weight on what they call credit utilization—how close you get to the borrowing limit of each of your accounts.

The Fair Isaac Company says that for optimal scoring, each account's outstanding credit should be no more than 50 percent of the credit line and hopefully less, preferably less than 30 percent of your total available credit. By the way, as you are paying down your balances, it is wise to focus first on the highest interest rate credit cards or loans. This will help reduce the overall amount of your payments that go toward interest and not toward principal reduction.

3. Set a credit report review schedule.

You have the right to get a copy of all three of your credit reports—from Experian, TransUnion, and Equifax—once a year, for free. These three companies are the major players in the credit-reporting world. You can get a free copy of your credit report by ordering them at www.annualcreditreport.com.

You may want to consider not ordering all three reports from each of the three companies all at the same time. By spreading out the dates you receive each of your credit reports, you'll get a continuous view of how your credit picture looks over time because the three credit bureaus feed each other the latest information on a continual basis. It is a good way to catch errors on your credit report and keep a steady watch for identity theft.

By the way, be careful with all those ads you may see that advertise free credit reports. Many of them will demand a credit card number from you, which means at some point, those reports won't be free. There are several websites that offer free or low-cost credit reports. Some even offer credit monitoring services to alert you about changes to your credit score. These monitoring services may charge a fee, but it might be worth it to stay on top of your credit reputation.

4. Pay on time and pay more than the minimum.

If you have been late with payments or have stuck only to paying the minimum payments, it's time to give that up now. Here is what you should do:

- **Plan ahead.** To avoid late payments, note the due dates when the bills arrive and then set a date for payment five to seven days ahead of those due dates so you will definitely be able to mail your payment on time.
- **Log on to pay.** Another option is to pay online. This payment method avoids a payment getting lost in the mail or arriving late. Many banks even offer guaranteed on-time payment schedules as a part of their online payment services.
- **Set up automatic payments.** Another option is to have payments made automatically from your bank account. Most credit card companies and many other lenders

offer this service, and most of the time, it is free. To put more toward reducing the balance, it may be time to do a budget or to fine-tune the budget you already have. This will help you identify the non-essential spending you have been doing so you can pay your outstanding credit balances even faster.

5. Cut up cards, but do not close the account.

Closing accounts—even those that have had zero balances for years—is generally a bad idea. Lenders want to see a long record of responsible credit management, and longtime accounts that you haven't touched in years may actually help your score because it shows you have some restraint in the use of credit.

- While maintaining longtime accounts, be aware that, increasingly, credit card companies are proactively closing accounts that have not been used in the last eighteen to twenty-four months.

To prevent an undesired "lack of use" closure of one of your accounts, create a schedule for using one of these non-primary accounts to make a small purchase periodically, maybe just to fill up the car, so that none of them go dormant.

6. Avoid no-documentation or low-documentation loans.

If you are self-employed or otherwise do not have a lot of easily verifiable income, you may have trouble getting a loan. A potential lender may demand you do a lot of extra work to get the documentation they need to approve your loan. If you are self-employed, be sure to keep good income records so you can document your income to a potential lender.

The bottom line here is that the days of easy credit are virtually gone. And they may not come this way again for a long, long time—if ever. Take the time to stay on top of your personal financial affairs. Use credit wisely. Seek guidance from a trained financial professional to help you keep your financial life on track so you can live your life on your terms.

CHAPTER 3

HOW SHOULD I BEGIN SAVING AND INVESTING?

Better than borrowing is using your own money. If you have implemented a smart budget and learned to live with it, you are going to find that things start to change for you. Not only will your life feel less chaotic, unprepared, and threatened by what comes next, but you will also realize that you are gaining in wealth.

But more money can also mean more trouble if you don't think ahead and start setting aside some of your gains.

Most people know they should save and invest some of their money, but they may not even know how to get started. Let's take a look at how you can lay an important foundation for your financial future.

THE RULES OF THRIFT.

First, let's talk about saving. In order to have any money to save, the first step is to learn to live on less than you earn. How much? Here's a useful little rule to live by:

1. Implement the 80 percent rule.

A good "rule of thumb" for most people is to learn to live on 80 percent of their net take-home pay. If you spend 110 percent of your net take-home, then you go deeper in debt. But if you get by on 80 percent of what you bring in, you'll be saving 20 percent of your net income. Every single time you spend less than you make, you get richer.

For some people who are currently living paycheck-to-paycheck, month-to-month, and ending up with more month than they have paychecks, the very idea of living on less could be daunting, to say the least. So, if you don't feel like you have any spare dollars to save, how do you get started?

2. Clip when you can't cut.

If you can't live on 80 percent of your net take-home, can you get by on 99 percent? Of course you can. Even if you start with just 1 percent of your income instead of 20 percent, you are making a start in the right direction. Everyone can set aside at least a dollar or two from time to time. Maybe you take a sandwich from home once or twice a week rather than eating out for lunch. The five or ten dollars you save each time you do this is money you can now put into your savings account.

The lesson is simple: if you can't cut 20 percent from your take-home, start with a baby step—let's say by getting by on that 99 percent *and* by clipping coupons to save money at the grocery store—and using what you save to fund your first savings account deposit. Saving is a way of living. It doesn't have to be difficult or painful. It just requires a little thoughtfulness and planning. Clipping a coupon isn't exactly heavy lifting. Using a coupon when you buy something you would buy anyway is the very definition of "free money."

3. Make saving a habit.

Once you have started saving, look for new ways to add to what you can save each week or each month. Study your normal household expenses and look for ways to save a little here and there to grow and nurture your savings account.

So skip the expensive restaurant meals, wash your own car, and don't spend money on a movie you already know is bad. Keep doing this until you reach your target savings rate of saving 20 percent of your net income.

4. Build an emergency savings account.

Your first savings goal should be to have an emergency savings account equal to about three to six months worth of living expenses. If you have been closely watching and tracking your spending habits and looking for savings opportunities, you should know about how much you are spending each month to support your lifestyle. Go back and look at that budget of yours. This monthly spending amount is very important to know to help you plan for your long-term financial future.

Once you have three to six months in cash savings readily accessible should you really need it, you have established an important foundation for your financial future. You have taken the first step toward financial freedom and financial independence.

. . .

Next, we will look at what comes after laying the proper financial foundation of building savings that equals three to six months of living expenses. We will talk about getting started with investing to help your savings grow and set you on your path to financial peace of mind.

CHAPTER 4

HOW CAN I GROW MY SAVINGS?

Once you have accumulated a cash reserve equal to three to six months' worth of your living expenses, you are ready to begin the journey of potentially making your savings grow.

This chapter describes how to make investments that will make your money work as hard for you as you did to earn it in the first place. But remember, *any method of increasing wealth involves risk*. The trick is controlling those risks.

The word "investment" can conjure up all sorts of images, depending on your experiences and frames of reference. Here is a concept that may help you to organize your thoughts about how to approach structuring your investments.

Architecturally, a pyramid is one of the strongest structures that has ever been built and provides a helpful metaphor for how we should consider structuring our investments.

A Simple Investment Risk Pyramid

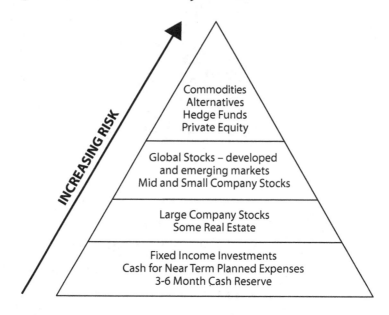

Foundation: At the very base of the pyramid, we would put our most secure and safest investments. One important part of this foundation is the three to six months of cash reserves we accumulated to protect us from having to worry so much about life's little emergencies. To this we would add funds we will need in the near term for planned expenditures, such as a new car, room addition, vacation, etc. Also in this foundational tier would be income-oriented investments, including fixed-income investments such as certificates of deposit, treasury bonds, corporate bonds, municipal bonds, fixed-rate annuities, and then perhaps bonds of other kinds, such as government bonds issued by foreign governments outside the United States.

Moderate Risk: Following these relatively safe and secure income-oriented investments and further up the pyramid, we might consider investments in the stocks of big, well-established, financially strong companies. Certain kinds of real estate investments might fit in this layer as well. Mutual funds and exchange-traded funds of these kinds of securities would also fit in this category.

Higher Risk: Next, we might consider stocks in midsize companies and even smaller, emerging growth-type companies that are still expanding and growing at a faster pace than the larger, more well-established companies might be able to do. Again, mutual funds and exchange-traded funds that own stocks of these companies would also fit in this category.

Highest Risk: As we approach the top of the pyramid, if appropriate, some investors may consider more exotic and higher-risk investments that offer an even greater potential return on our money. Investments in this category are subject to substantial amount of risk and liquidity concerns. As such, these investments may not be appropriate for most investors. This category might include investments in commodities, alternatives, hedge funds, private equity, and so on.

Notice that as we move up the pyramid, we are taking progressively higher investment risks but doing so with progressively smaller amounts of our money. That way, if something doesn't turn out as well as expected with one of our higher-risk investments, the damage may be more tolerable.

A balanced investment plan might include all of the elements we mentioned here. However, the proportionate share of your money committed to any particular investment should be small.

This practice will limit any chances that the consequences of any investment's failure to perform as expected will knock our overall investment plan off track.

So, when you consider different possible ways to invest your savings, remember this "investment pyramid." Start with a strong foundation of adequate cash reserves. Build on that foundation with more-conservative investments in the beginning, and then consider gradually expanding your exposure to increasing levels of investment risk that provide a chance for a higher return if it is appropriate for you.

If you keep the investment pyramid in mind, you will have a handy guide to help you choose investments wisely while limiting risk.

CHAPTER 5

HOW CAN I TEACH MY CHILDREN HEALTHY SAVINGS HABITS?

Children who learn the importance of saving at a young age are much better prepared to manage their money independently once they are grown.

One of the most effective financial tools you can give a child is an appreciation for an emergency fund and the advice on how to build it themselves. An emergency fund should contain three to six months worth of money to cover living expenses—its main focus should cover all loss of income, not just a car payment or a refrigerator repair. With people losing jobs and college expenses continuing to grow, the younger you can get your child started, the better. You'll find some of this is similar to the grown-up model.

TEN WAYS TO HELP YOUR CHILD BUILD A LIFETIME EMERGENCY FUND

1. Start by encouraging them to save something, no matter how small the amount.

Even if it is a few cents out of an allowance, a teenager should be encouraged to set up a separate savings or checking account—some place not easy to access—where they can house the money.

Interest-bearing accounts are better. For young children, piggy banks work well. It's about setting goals and knowing where the money is.

2. Help them develop a balance between treats and sacrifices.

Financial independence requires a balance of risk and reward. Life can't be all about building reserves, so tell the teen when they hit a certain level for the fund—maybe a midpoint toward the three-month mark—they can treat themselves to clothes or an electronic device. After the purchase, they go right back to saving.

3. Encourage them to direct all change into the emergency fund.

No matter how old or young the child, it is a good idea to take non-essential funds and direct them toward the emergency fund. Change is a great way to get started. It sounds cliché, but pennies really do add up.

4. Set an example.

Does your child see you saving? Do you physically set aside money and talk about goals for that money? Your child sees and hears all of this. While parents can't be perfect, think about the money behaviors you are demonstrating in front of the kids, and try to make them positive.

5. Keep them away from credit as long as possible.

It is one thing for a teenager to use their parents' credit card while they are still living at home. It is quite another when they get their first taste of freedom hundreds of miles away. Parents may co-sign the student's credit card but keep it in the student's name. That way, parents will know when financial missteps occur; this will be a strong incentive for the student to keep his credit rating clean while the parents are watching over his actions.

6. Set up money meetings.

Whether the child is living at home or off at school, it makes sense for the parent and child to have a few meetings during the year to talk about the range of money issues the child is facing, and during that time, the emergency fund can be up for inspection and discussion.

7. Make them set up a real budget.

Budgeting comes with saving. Young kids can do their first budget on paper—they can track what they spend and save over a month or two and then establish what comfortable amounts for both will be, just as you did. Teens and prospective college students might find it useful to have personal finance software to track their everyday expenses. Again, review these details during your money meetings.

8. Get them interested in better-paying, safe savings vehicles.

At some point, the piggy bank has to go. An emergency fund can eventually gravitate to other interest-bearing accounts that might pay more but only as long as the money stays liquid. If the emergency fund is healthy, it is also wise for parents to talk to their children about setting up their first IRAs to get a jump on retirement planning and considerable tax savings.

9. Remind them that today's emergency fund may not fit next year's needs.

An emergency fund will almost always need to expand in size as the person ages: more years, more expenses, more emergencies. Make time to discuss with your child why emergency funds should change with life circumstances.

10. Train them to start saving tax refunds.

If Uncle Sam kicks back a few bucks, then by all means, put it in the emergency fund or other savings vehicles. Helping your child develop sound money habits will pay off for their entire life. Helping them develop a lifetime emergency fund will go a long way toward helping your child have a life that is freer from money worries. It will take some effort on your part, but the results can be rewarding.

CHAPTER 6

HOW CAN I HELP MY CHILD OR GRANDCHILD SAVE FOR COLLEGE?

There are two facts about a college education that most parents and grandparents understand only too well.

First, college is increasingly becoming a prerequisite for success. College graduates earn nearly twice as much as those with only a high school diploma.

Second, college can, to say the least, be an expensive proposition. Over the past ten years, the average total cost of college has risen more than twice as fast as the consumer price index.

So, if you want to help a child or grandchild save for college, what are your options? While there are many college-savings strategies available, 529 plans offer many unique advantages.

CHILDREN'S EDUCATION ACCOUNTS—529 PLANS

What Is a 529 Plan?

529 plans offer a flexible, tax-advantaged vehicle to save for a child's college education. They offer federal and, in some cases, state income tax advantages that help make it possible to grow

your college savings faster than in a taxable account. You pay no taxes on earnings while your money remains in a 529 account.

When your child or grandchild is ready to enter college, withdrawals are exempt from federal income taxes when used for qualified higher education expenses, such as tuition, fees, certain room and board costs, and supplies.

Parents and grandparents or anyone else can make contributions to a 529 plan account. Your gifts to the account can help reduce your gross estate under current estate and gift tax rules. As owner of the account, you remain in control of the funds and determine when and how the money actually gets spent.

If the designated child does not need all the money for his or her education, you can change the beneficiary and use the money for a different child or other family member. Furthermore, if you need the money for some other purpose, you can withdraw some or all of the balance at any time. However, if you withdraw money for a purpose other than educational expenses, the withdrawal may be subject to income taxes.

529 plans are not the only college savings option, but they are a sound option to consider.

Disclosure: An investor should consider the investment objectives, risks, charges and expenses associated with 529 plans before investing. Most states offer their own 529 programs which may provide advantages and benefits exclusively for their residents and taxpayers. The tax implications of a 529 plan should be discussed with a qualified tax advisor.

FINANCE 101:
Laying the Foundation

II. PLANNING BASICS

Surveys show that a majority of Americans feel that having a personal financial plan is important. The reality, however, is that many Americans spend more time planning their next vacation than they do planning their personal financial affairs. A shockingly small percentage actually has a written financial plan.

There are many reasons that a financial plan is important for just about everyone. There is an old saying attributed to Yogi Berra: "If you don't know where you are going, you'll end up someplace else." Well, it is certainly true with financial issues.

The idea of having a plan before starting an important project is not new. We do it all the time in other areas of our lives. Most sensible people would not start building a house without a set of plans to guide the process, and most people would not take a long car trip without a map to direct them on their way.

A well-thought-out personal financial plan can provide an ongoing framework for making intelligent decisions about your money and financial affairs as you travel down life's pathway.

CHAPTER 7

HOW DO I BEGIN DEVELOPING A PERSONAL FINANCIAL PLAN?

Getting your financial affairs in order is no small task. We are all busy, and our financial affairs are not always at the forefront of our thoughts. However, whether you are fully squared away or teetering on the brink of a serious financial mess, the best place to start is to begin with the end in mind.

Steven R. Covey talks about this concept in his iconic book *The 7 Habits of Highly Effective People.* If you have a clear vision of your ultimate destination, figuring out how to get there becomes much easier. On the other hand, if you lack clarity about where you are headed, how will you know where to start? How would you even know if you are making progress toward your goal?

Complete the initial steps below as you begin developing your personal financial plan:

1. Ask yourself some searching questions—the kind that help you to examine what is truly important to you about your money. So, what is important about money to you? Is it a sense of security? Maybe a sense of comfort? Or perhaps it may be the peace of mind that comes from knowing deep inside that everything is going to be OK. Whatever you value, whatever is important to you in your life, it is vitally important that you think it through. A trained, caring financial professional may be a great help to ask the right questions to help you gain clarity about your future.

- If you want to plan for retirement, when would you like to retire?
- How much income will you need?
- What about your family? If you want to provide for the education of your children or grandchildren, what type of school did you have in mind? Public or private? Local or out of state? Ivy League or your own alma mater?
- If you want to buy a lake or beach house or a retirement getaway, where do you want it to be? How much will it cost?
- Think out the details: What other accouterments will be needed? If your dream home is a lakefront cottage, will you need to acquire furnishings or buy a boat? And where will you dock that boat?

2. Determine your goals. Goals are very useful tools, but, as with any tool, you have to know how to use them. Here are some pointers I have found helpful:

Here are five sample questions that you can use to start developing financial goals for your life. In thinking about answers, look at your short-term *and* long-term goals—and be specific about what you really want.

- **Is your goal specific?** It is important that your goals be *measurable* and quantifiable. If you want to retire at a certain age, what income will you need to support the retirement lifestyle you imagine? Many experts suggest that most will live comfortably on 70 to 80 percent of their pre-retirement income. Study your budget and how you are spending money now. This will give you clues to help you estimate how much income you will need in retirement. State your income requirements in today's dollars, as if you were spending the money today. Factoring in inflation and taxes will come later.

- **Is your goal realistic?** Your goals should be *achievable*. If you are a younger person making plans for retirement, you probably have enough time to build toward your goal. If you are older and planning to retire soon, that may present some challenges. I recall a gentleman who came to my office early in my career. He was fifty-seven years old, had $15,000 in savings, made $40,000 a year in salary, and wanted to retire at sixty with a $50,000 per year income. These goals could not pass the realistic and achievable test!

- **Do you have time to realize your goals?** Stating your goals should also include a reference to *time*. When do you want to see these goals happen? Education costs for college usually start about age eighteen. That might be easy. But retiring at fifty-five might require different preparation than retiring at seventy years of age.

- **Do you have a plan for achieving your goals?** With a clear vision of what you want and why you want it, you have laid an important foundation. Now you are ready to begin the process of creating a written plan to achieve your goals and make your dreams come true. Note that

I said "written plan." Just having ideas in your head is not enough. It is important to get them out and on paper. You wouldn't start to build a house without a set of blueprints. A written financial plan is your blueprint for building your future.

CHAPTER 8

WHAT SHOULD MY PERSONAL FINANCIAL PLAN INCLUDE?

No matter where you are on your financial journey, your personal financial plan should include the following:

1. Risk management.

This involves reviewing your insurance coverage to make sure that you are adequately protected from a major financial disaster. Look at your homeowner's insurance, automobile coverage, and umbrella liability coverage. Make sure that you know what is covered and what is not covered. You should understand that you are, essentially, self-insuring anything that your policy doesn't cover.

Proper risk management also includes looking at disability insurance, life insurance, health insurance, and long-term care insurance. Some people's situations may call for exploring other types of risk management issues, but the ones I have mentioned will cover it for most people.

2. Estate-planning.

Review documents such as your wills, trusts, durable powers of attorney, living wills, and health care proxy statements. If you do not already have these important documents, then this is the time to take care of putting them in place.

3. Taxes.

Take a close look at your income tax returns and the tax-planning strategies you have in place. (And if they aren't in place, consult with a tax professional.) Paying income taxes is a part of life for most Americans, but nothing in the tax code requires that you pay *more* than is legally required. Looking for opportunities to save on taxes can be a great money-saving exercise.

4. Investments.

Make sure you understand your investments, your investment goals, your cash reserves, your asset allocation strategy, your risk tolerance, and much more.

5. Retirement planning.

Explore your employer's retirement plan to make sure that you are taking full advantage of it, and make sure that you are properly invested to meet your personal needs and goals. What will you need for a happy retirement? Are you thinking about working part time in retirement? Will you have other sources of income in retirement, such as Social Security or pension payments?

An effective personal financial plan must address each of these five critical areas. Do you have a plan in place? Is it in writing? Does it address all five areas? Do you review the plan and your progress on a frequent basis? If you can't answer these questions with a confident *"Yes!"*, then it may be time to consider developing a personal financial plan to help guide you in reaching your financial goals.

CHAPTER 9

HOW DO I LOCATE A QUALIFIED FINANCIAL PLANNER?

Most people wouldn't dream of building a house without a plan. And most people would go to a professional to help create that plan. So if you are like most people, you probably will need some professional help to get this plan right. While there are financial planning tools and software available for the do-it-yourselfer, I do not recommend taking that route. At the risk of sounding self-serving for those in the financial planning profession, most people are just not equipped with adequate knowledge and training to get financial planning right working entirely on their own.

1. Look for someone who is a CERTIFIED FINANCIAL PLANNER™ professional, a CFP®. The initials are more than just a jumble of letters. To use the CFP® designation, a professional must have the met the CFP Board of Standards certification for education, examination, experience, and ethics. Just as you might not want your new house to be planned by somebody who isn't an accredited architect, getting a CFP® on your side in the planning process may be a sensible step.

2. Ask family and friends, especially those with financial circumstances and lifestyles similar to your own. Also ask professionals you trust, such as your attorney or your CPA. They often know who is really good and who is not. When you have assembled a few names, do an online search with Google or other search engine and see what you find. Check them out on social media. See how they present themselves and what demographic they seem to be targeting.

3. Look on industry websites such as the Financial Planning Association (www.fpanet.org) or the CFP Board's website (www.cfp.net). You will find a great deal of valuable information there and a simple search engine request will lead you to find a CFP® in your area. Before committing, go to the CFP Board's site to see if the advisor's CFP® status is in good standing.

4. Verify a potential financial planner's regulatory history by visiting the Financial Industry Regulatory Authority's (FINRA) BrokerCheck website and the Security and Exchange Commission's website "Investment Adviser Public Disclosure" page. This is all common-sense due diligence, but once you feel certain the advisor's regulatory background is clear, you are ready to set up some initial interviews to check them out in person.

CHAPTER 10

WHAT QUESTIONS SHOULD I ASK BEFORE SELECTING A FINANCIAL PLANNER?

Before selecting a financial planner, be sure to ask the following questions:

1. What is your educational history, and what are your professional credentials?

Ask about licenses they hold and what other professional credentials they may have besides the right to call themselves a CFP®. For financial planning work, hiring a professional with that designation may be a helpful resource. An Investment Adviser Representative (IAR) of a Registered Investment Adviser (RIA) will be acting in a fiduciary capacity when they work with you. This is an important distinction and one worth learning about. Many financial professionals in practice today operate under a different standard, referred to as a suitability standard. I will cover this suitability vs. fiduciary issue later in this chapter.

2. What services do you provide, and what services does your firm provide?

What you are looking for here is an assurance that they are customarily offering financial planning services as a regular part of their business practice. Some firms only offer financial planning help. Some offer investment management services. Some do both and offer other services as well.

3. What type of compensation do you receive? A commission or a fee?

You're looking to determine the rules and regulations that guide their practice.

Suitability standard. When a financial services professional sells a commission based product,, the professional is held to a standard called *suitability*. He or she must determine if the investment product is suitable for the client. In the brokerage world, the product need only be suitable for the client for the sale to be acceptable. The focus of the rules and regulations for brokers is on *responsibility to the brokerage firm employing the financial services professional.*.

Fiduciary standard. On the other hand, if the financial services professional charges a fee based on advice, the professional is then held to a fiduciary standard. A fiduciary must act in the best interests of his or her client and is held to the "prudent man rule." The "prudent man rule" says that an advisor must know the client's situation well enough to advise the client to act in a prudent manner, to do what any prudent person would do, given the same circumstances. In other words, *the best interests of the client have to come first*, before the interests of the advisor or the advisory firm that employs him or her. That is a very different standard of care than the suitability standard found in the brokerage world.

For the past few years, and especially after the 2008 financial meltdown, there has been quite a debate in Washington about expanding the fiduciary standard to cover brokers, but many in the brokerage world have opposed such a move. Clearly, the fiduciary standard is a higher standard of care. So, when it comes to working with a financial professional, would you rather get advice from someone who is bound to rules requiring they act in your best interests and advise you in a prudent manner, or would you buy an investment product from someone who is only required to determine if what they are recommending is suitable for you?

4. How do you charge for your services? What other forms of compensation might you receive if I/we do business with you?

Some professionals charge an initial planning fee as a single, stand-alone engagement. Some charge an asset management fee expressed as a percentage of assets being managed. Some charge a fixed retainer fee. Some might have soft dollar arrangements. Some will make additional money by selling you a product or service, thus providing a potential incentive to steer their recommendations toward the products and services they have to sell.

5. What types of clients do you prefer to specialize in? What is your ideal client profile?

Many professionals specialize in working with only a narrow specialty type of client. Ideally, you want to choose an advisor who regularly works with people like you so they will be familiar with the issues you are likely to face over the course of time.

6. How much contact do you have with your clients on an ongoing basis?

Once a written financial plan is prepared and presented to you and you have all your questions answered, the next step will be to implement the plan. Ideally, you will want a caring professional to help implement the plan properly, with an understanding of the way it was designed. Longer term, you will want ongoing help and guidance to keep the plan on track. Ask if you will work with the CFP® professional specifically, individually, or if they use a team approach where you will interact with several people over time.

7. What can I expect if I am your client? What makes your client experience unique from other professionals? Why should I choose you to be my financial advisor?

The bottom line is, "Why would I want to work with you?" Let them tell you what makes them different and why you should choose them.

8. Ask yourself: Who did all the talking?

If you asked all the questions and did most of the talking, you may not have the right advisor for you. Ideally, you want a dialogue.

You want them to show a genuine interest in you. They should be asking you questions about you, your family, your life, your dreams, goals, and vision for your future. If they do not seem interested in you, why would you want to have a relationship with them? Ask yourself, "Is this a person I can trust? Is this a person I can work with over time?" If the answer is yes, then you may have found a CERTIFIED FINANCIAL PLANNER™ professional who can be your financial partner to help you build your future.

FROM OUR FILES...
Is It Worth Getting a Second Opinion?

Financial advisors are similar to doctors in that they do not object to clients who seek a second opinion on an important decision. Let me share a fictional story of Susan, who was the wife of a very well-respected and well-known physician. Her husband had always taken care of their financial affairs—handling investment decisions and working with estate-planning attorneys, insurance agents, and other advisors and service providers. Susan had not been very involved at all with these issues and was perfectly happy with that situation. She had other interests.

Then one evening, she heard something that caused her to begin to wonder if she and her husband were as well taken care of as she had always believed. She was attending a program at her church when she heard a financial advisor speak on financial and estate-planning topics. It took about a year for her husband and her to decide to seek a second opinion, but they finally did.

They contacted the financial advisor to set an appointment to discuss their situation. After meeting with them, the financial advisor recommended that they do a thorough review of their financial, estate, risk management, and retirement planning. After the advisor completed the review and presented his findings, he was able to tell them that the good news was that they had done a very good job managing their affairs. They were very well set to achieve both their short- and long-term goals—that is, if nothing went wrong.

There were some gaping holes in their insurance coverage, exposing them to serious risks that they had not fully considered. There were missing pieces to their estate plan that would have meant problems for the remaining family members in settling their estate once they had passed on. And there was a risk they could run out of money if they both lived a very long time because of how they had invested compared to how they were spending their money.

While all of these issues were potentially devastating, every one of them could still be addressed and corrected. The financial advisor pointed out that if they took appropriate action on each item, it could go a long way to eliminating or at least reducing the formerly unknown risk factors.

Susan and her husband chose to return to their long-time advisors to execute remedies for the issues that had been uncovered in our work together. They were appreciative to have uncovered hidden risks and issues they were not aware of. Susan was especially grateful for an impartial second opinion that helped to settle nagging doubts she had harbored for some time. For Susan, getting a second opinion was valuable indeed.

CHAPTER 11

HOW OFTEN SHOULD I UPDATE MY PERSONAL FINANCIAL PLAN?

This part of the book has been all about developing a plan—one that is written down, one you feel accurately reflects your goals, and one that allows for the participation of a professional ally, such as a CFP® professional, should you feel it necessary. Congratulations! The fact that you even have a written financial plan at all sets you apart from the crowd.

However, a plan is worth nothing without careful implementation and tracking your progress. In fact, tracking progress should be part of the plan. The tips below will help you pay attention to changing circumstances and how they might affect your plan.

1. Monitor financial laws.

As Mark Twain pointed out, "No man's life, liberty, or property are safe while the legislature is in session." Congress can meet and change the rules. Will a tax law change or other development affect your financial plan?

2. Respond to personal change.

The following life events, and others not mentioned here, can affect your financial plan:

- a new job or career change
- a new child or grandchild
- the purchase or sale of a home
- a marriage or divorce
- the death of a relative

3. Review your plan at least annually.

We recommend our clients review their financial plans and the progress they are making toward their goals regularly. You should do the same. But all that progress can be ambushed when tragedy strikes or when things take an unexpected turn.

Now, let's take a deeper look at key areas that must be addressed in your financial planning, starting with ways to help protect yourself from unanticipated changes.

FINANCE 102:
Common Scenario Planning

I. PLANNING FOR UNEXPECTED CHANGE

Life happens 24/7, and it is rarely predictable, which is why it's so important to consider what could happen and plan accordingly. For most of us, protection from unplanned events comes in the form of insurance, so it's important to evaluate how your coverage fits into your overall plan.

CHAPTER 12

DO I HAVE THE RIGHT INSURANCE COVERAGE?

If you are like most people, you have insurance on your home and insurance on your automobiles. You may have had this coverage in place for a number of years. You may have been dealing with the same insurance agent for all of that time. That insurance agent likely completes the application forms for renewal of coverage, hands it to you for signature, and asks you for a check to pay the premium. Most people are so used to dealing with the same agent and the same insurance company year after year that they never stop to really look at the terms buried deep in the fine print of the policy.

Here are a few pointers that will help you evaluate your policy and determine if any changes are necessary:

1. Determine your policy exclusions and limitations. What are you covered for and how much does the insurance company pay in the event of a loss? Maybe even more importantly, what risks are you *not* covered for? We call these policy exclusions and limitations of coverage. These issues can become critical in the event of a loss—but by the time you have a loss, it is too late to make any changes to your coverage.

Find out if you have actual cash value coverage or replacement cost coverage on your home and the contents in it. The difference can be substantial. Actual cash value coverage will only pay the depreciated cost of the item, whereas replacement cost coverage covers the cost of replacing the lost item in a similar product at current values.

For example, if you have a lightening strike and a ten-year-old television goes out as a result, replacement cost coverage will get you a new TV of a similar size and features, in a currently available model. Actual cash value coverage will pay you the value of a ten-year-old TV, which is very little, and then you are on your own to replace the TV.

2. Have your policies reviewed at least every three years *and* every time you make a major change, such as purchasing a new car or adding on to your home.

Have your insurance agent review each policy with you and explain specifically what is covered and for how much and just as importantly, what specifically is not covered.

Here is a helpful review checklist:

- Ask about your options to add upgrades to your policy that would fill in any gaps you discover in the review process, such as changed property values or personal changes you would like to make.
- Make sure you have an up-to-the-minute list of things that have changed or been added (or taken away) that might affect your coverage plan.
- Ask to see a copy of the application form you are to sign to make sure that the application form is filled out

completely and correctly. The form must accurately reflect the policy provisions you have chosen. Do not just assume your agent has done his homework and filled out the form correctly.

- Make sure that what you agreed on is actually on the form. Make this three-year review a part of your ongoing routine.

If you ever have a loss, you will be glad you invested the time to be clear about your actual coverage and what you need—and what to expect.

3. Make sure you have the proper automotive coverage. *Ask about coverage for uninsured motorists.* If you are in an accident and the other party does not have insurance, this coverage can be invaluable for making sure you are taken care of properly.

Also ask about *diminishment of value coverage.* As you probably are aware, automobiles are a quickly depreciating asset. If you buy a brand new car and drive it off the dealer's lot and then later that week have a wreck, your car is now a used car and not a new car and, therefore, your car has lost value. There are now insurance companies that will cover that loss and get you back into a brand new car.

Another aspect of this concept of diminishment of value is if you are in a wreck and the car is repaired, the fact that your car has been in a wreck will diminish its value when you go to trade it in. If you have diminishment of value coverage, you may be able to recover most or all of that value loss. You should be aware that insurance companies are sometimes reluctant to talk about this coverage, but it is available and worth considering.

4. Review your homeowners' policy. Another important consideration is the exclusions in your homeowners' policy. Do you know what is *not* covered? If you want peace of mind, you should know. You may find that certain items, such as jewelry, furs, collections, art, computers, etc., may have specific limits or even exclusions as to how much coverage the insurance company will allow under the base homeowners' policy. Most of the time, these gaps can be addressed with a personal articles rider, or it may be a separate policy, depending on the insurance company. For these situations, you would list those specific items and cover them separately from the base homeowners' policy.

If you live in a part of the country that might be at risk for earthquakes, you may want to consider earthquake coverage. For example, my home in Arkansas is close to the New Madrid Fault. Some scientists believe that it is only a matter of time before we will see a major earthquake event in or near our area. So, I purchased earthquake coverage to protect my home. Your base homeowners' coverage typically does not cover earthquake damage at all. There are many insurance products that provide ways of covering these kinds of localized risks. Flood insurance is an example. Do you live in the tornado belt or on the Gulf coast? Think about that.

Another insurance consideration is an *umbrella liability policy*. Your base homeowners and automobile policies designate a certain amount of liability coverage. For example, a typical homeowner's policy has about $300,000 of liability coverage. Yet, if someone were to sue you regarding an accident that happened at your home, the potential court judgments might be much higher than $300,000. An umbrella liability policy extends the limits of your base policies to $1,000,000 or more. Many of my clients carry $2 or $3 million in coverage, some even more. While I think this kind of extended coverage is important for most everyone, it is especially important if you are in a high-visibility, high-risk profession or live in an "affluent" neighborhood where there may be presumptions about your personal wealth. Similarly, an "open perils" policy will give you greater peace of mind than a "named perils" policy. Insurance is all about taking care of problems you never expected.

CHAPTER 13

HOW DO I RESPOND IN THE EVENT OF A HEALTH CRISIS?

Dealing with an expensive family health care crisis can be challenging, especially if it is one caused by a frightening and potentially life-threatening diagnosis for which you do not feel adequately prepared. But you can get through this kind of emergency. Stay as calm as you can, and focus on dealing with the crisis in a responsible way. Take each of the following eight steps one at a time.

1. It's not all about the money.

If you or someone you love is sick, of course you will want to obtain the best care possible, not just what your bank account and health insurance can buy. Talk with a qualified financial professional who has experience in dealing with health care issues. They can help you assess your financial situation against various goals for retirement, your expenses, your children's education, and other matters.

2. Grill the patient's insurance agent or HR person.

If you or family members have bought health insurance through an agent or your employer, insist that they explain *exactly* what the plan covers and where your deductibles do and do not apply. Generally, a serious illness will quickly require full outlay of the policy's deductible. This is where your emergency fund is important. Pay attention to how much the insurance will pay and how much you will pay out of pocket above and beyond the deductible, an amount often referred to as the "patient's co-insurance."

3. Check on experimental treatment and see how it will affect coverage.

If the diagnosis is cancer or some other potentially life-threatening illness, you may want to research medical centers offering clinical trials beyond the tried and true treatments. When doing so, keep in mind that some insurance plans might look askance at certain treatments that could potentially lead to other health issues. Use caution in these matters, but if the insurer approves, see if such experimental treatment can get you a break on costs.

4. Get those directives in order.

A *health care advance directive* provides written instructions for doctors to follow in case you or your family members are incapacitated. The most commonly known health care directive is a do-not-resuscitate (DNR) order. Another is a health care power of attorney that designates a particular individual—a spouse, a friend, an adult child—to carry out your medical wishes if you cannot speak for yourself. Meanwhile, financial powers of attorney designate an individual to handle financial affairs if the sick or deceased cannot do it for themselves. Be sure to consult with a qualified attorney, as each state has its own requirements.

5. If you have no will or complete estate plan, make one.

A will does not have to be enormously detailed to relieve problems for survivors, but it can create enormous problems if it doesn't exist. If there is no executed will, the estate is intestate, which means that property is distributed by state laws. Yet, beyond getting or reviewing a will, it makes even more sense to review all of your assets to determine if more-detailed directives or trusts are necessary and, most importantly, to make sure beneficiaries on insurance, retirement accounts, and other investments are up to date. See more later in this book on the subject of estate-planning.

6. Consider whether you can make monetary support a gift.

It is good to get tax and financial advice on making a one-time gift to support a patient. Would the potential loss of money injure you, and worse, would it injure the relationship? If you do not think you will be repaid, are you willing to consider it a gift?

7. Ask for generics and samples.

Many physicians are willing to recommend a generic substitute or at least supply you with a few samples of the drug they are already prescribing. While doctors can't get away with passing out sample drugs to all their patients, always ask. As long as they are prescribing the medication, samples with the proper dosage can provide cost savings to patients.

8. Begin negotiations before there is a financial problem.

The best time to speak with the hospital business office isn't when you are behind on your payments. Once a diagnosis is made, either you or someone you designate as your agent needs to contact the hospital business office to check on payment schedules and possible discount plans if you are uninsured or fear your insurance may not cover a significant portion of costs. Any creditor appreciates a customer who is willing to come to the table first, and some hospitals have funds available for certain situations.

Remember, you are not the first person to ever have dealt with a health care crisis. You can get through it. Many others have. Do the best you can—that is all anyone could ask.

CHAPTER 14

WHAT ABOUT DISABILITY
AND LIFE INSURANCE?

Disability insurance is not the same as health insurance. Disability insurance protects your income if you become sick or injured and are unable to work and the injury or illness could mean an interruption to your regular income. While we recommend that clients keep three to six months of living expenses as a readily available cash reserve, some illnesses or injuries might require a longer period of recovery. What can you do to replace the income that you are not able to produce any longer? For many people, the answer is disability insurance.

Disability insurance can be purchased as an individual policy directly from an insurance company. Many employers offer disability insurance as an employee benefit option. Most policies, including employer plans, will replace about two-thirds of your normal income. On the surface this may sound like enough, since you are used to giving up a portion of your gross income to taxes. However, how the disability policy is purchased can affect how meaningful the benefit will be to you if you are sick or injured.

If you purchase a disability policy directly from an insurance company and pay the premiums out of your own pocket, the benefits paid by the policy are free from federal income tax under current tax law. On the other hand, if the very same coverage, even with the same insurance company, were offered as an employee benefit and your employer paid the premium, the same disability benefit would be paid to you as a taxable benefit. This could make a huge difference in how well the benefit payments did their job of replacing your working income.

If you are offered disability insurance by your employer, chances are it is something you should consider taking advantage of. Be sure to ask about how the premiums are paid to determine the income tax treatment of the benefit. Again, if you pay the premium out of your pocket, the benefits are paid free from federal income tax. If your employer pays the premium and takes a tax deduction for them as an employee benefit cost, your benefits will be paid to you as a taxable stream of income. Many savvy employers will handle payroll accounting so that it shows you paying the disability premiums from your income in order to make the benefit tax-free.

Life insurance provides cash to your beneficiaries at your death. For a younger person, purchasing life insurance can create an "instant estate" that you have not yet had time to save and accumulate. This money can provide for your family if you were to die prematurely. Another role life insurance can play is to provide cash for meeting a specific need in the event of a premature death. For example, a life insurance policy could be taken out to pay off a mortgage on your home or other property. The death benefit proceeds might be earmarked to provide a specified amount to cover educational costs for children or grandchildren.

How much life insurance to buy and how to buy it are important questions. There are many forms of life insurance policies offered today. At one end of the continuum is *simple term life* insurance. This is generally the lowest cost way to buy life insurance coverage. The term life premium is based on the pure cost of insuring the risk of death in a given year. The younger and healthier you are, the lower the premium. As you get older, the premium goes up accordingly, until later in life when the premiums can become prohibitively expensive. If you will need life insurance coverage for a very long time or perhaps the balance of your lifetime, term coverage may not be a good choice.

On the other end of the life insurance continuum is *whole life* insurance. With whole life, you pay a substantially higher premium than with term life. The extra amount of premium that you pay over and above the actual cost of insurance in a given year is held in a side account usually referred to as the cash value of the life insurance policy. This cash value builds up over time and eventually reaches a point where it is used to cover a portion of the cost of insurance later in life. Think of whole life insurance as a term policy with a side savings account to help pay the premiums as you age.

Between term and life is a whole host of other life insurance products with names like universal life, ten-, twenty-, or thirty-year term life, and many more. Some financial professionals will recommend buying term life and then creating your own savings or investment account to invest the difference in what you would have paid for whole life. Other professionals will recommend buying whole life and try to sell you on the benefits of a "tax advantaged" buildup of cash value inside the life insurance policy. Some policies will even have investment options for you to choose how you want your cash value invested.

There is probably no right or wrong answer regarding how to buy life insurance. But here are two concepts to keep in mind that may be helpful.

- *If your need for life insurance is temporary,* that is less than your entire lifetime, then term insurance will probably be your best bet.
- *If your need is more likely to be permanent,* that is your entire lifetime, then whole life or some variation will probably be a better fit.

A qualified financial professional can help you make sound decisions in this area.

Once you've purchased your life insurance policy, don't forget to assign your beneficiary designations. Many people don't think too much about the importance of beneficiary designations on life insurance. They will often list a spouse or a child as a beneficiary and do so without even giving the matter a second thought.

Know who your beneficiary is. The problem with this is that, in many cases, there are legal issues to be considered when choosing beneficiaries for life insurance policies. Even if the choice for naming a beneficiary was a well-informed choice at the time, it is important to keep the policies up to date with changing circumstances.

For example, we often find people have life insurance policies they have owned for a very long time and haven't actually looked at the policy in many years. When we do a review of their policies, we discover things like an ex-spouse or even a deceased person still named as a beneficiary. Or we find a minor child named as a beneficiary.

The owner of the life insurance policy typically has the power to change a beneficiary, and usually it is a fairly easy process. The policy owner asks for a change of beneficiary form. The form is completed and submitted to the insurance company, and the change is made. It is usually as simple as that. If your situation is more complex, you may want to consult your attorney for guidance on how to set up your beneficiaries.

Life insurance can be a valuable financial tool to provide cash to meet a variety of needs. Why not take a few moments to check that the insurance you are paying for will end up in the hands of those you intended?

There's more for you on this important topic in the chapter devoted to retirement planning. (See page 177.)

CHAPTER 15

WHAT SHOULD I KNOW ABOUT LONG-TERM CARE?

Long-term care is an important subject that is full of potential complications.

As we are living longer and longer, the chances of requiring long-term care increase. That's why this issue has been growing in importance, especially in the last ten to twenty years.

Health care facilities other than hospitals have many different names, such as rehabilitation center, long-term convalescent center, nursing home, and so on. *None of these other care facilities are technically hospitals.* Instead, they fall into a broad category called "long-term care." If you need long-term care, Medicare will pay for some or all of the cost for a very short period of time.

If your care needs extend beyond the time limits imposed by Medicare, you are simply on your own to pay out of your own pocket for your continuing care.

The cost of facilities that fit in the category of long-term care can often cost $4,000 to $6,000 per month per person and sometimes even more, depending on the part of the country and the level of skilled care you are going to need. This kind of cost can make a big dent in any family's savings and investments, and these costs are rising rapidly—much faster than the rate of inflation on other goods and services.

So, what do you do? Talk to a financial professional who can help you come up with answers to questions like these: If you begin to pay out of your own pocket, how long will it be before you are dipping too far into your own funds such that you are putting the financial stability and care of your healthy spouse in jeopardy? How long before your long-term financial future takes on a whole new, perhaps darker, view? The cost of long-term care can be significant over time, and it can ruin, or at least damage, a lifetime of saving for a comfortable retirement.

What follows are long-term care issues that need to be considered by virtually everyone.

1. Uncle Sam's in the picture for older Americans.

When most Americans reach age sixty-five, your health care insurance is going to be the government's Medicare program. With Medicare, you will then be subject to the government's rules on your health care. You will likely find these new rules to be quite different than what you may have been used to with other health care insurance coverage.

2. Medicare supplement insurance is offered by many private insurance carriers.

One key fact you need to be aware of is that the Medicare rules on your health care are the main driver of what is covered by your Medicare supplement policy. Here is how it works:

- **Supplementary coverage can be determined by Medicare coverage.** Medicare becomes your primary health care insurance at age sixty-five. If you purchase a Medicare supplement policy from a private insurance carrier, the supplement will help pay your co-pays, deductibles, and co-insurance related to your Medicare coverage. In other words, if Medicare covers it, generally the supplement policy will help with the co-pays, deductibles, and co-insurance related to your Medicare claim. However, if Medicare does not cover something, generally neither will your Medicare supplement policy.

- **Your supplement policy may offer some other benefits not covered by Medicare**, but for the most part, the supplement policy serves to be a support to your Medicare coverage. If your health care need is not covered by Medicare or your supplement policy, you are on your own to pay for your care out of your own pocket.

- **In the government's Medicare program, there is something called "diagnostic related groups" or "DRGs."** The DRGs are the government rules about your health care. There are more than four hundred DRGs, and each is very specific on its rules for that particular condition or illness. The government's rules spell out exactly when you are considered to be sick, exactly what procedures are appropriate for you to get well, and exactly how long you can be in the hospital to receive this approved care. If you don't do your part and get well on time, the hospital and the doctors involved ultimately have no choice but to move you out of the hospital to some other care facility.

- **For the most part, Medicare does not cover long-term care costs for very long.** After that, you are on your own to pay for your care out of your own pocket until you are completely out of money. At that point, the government will step back in and take care of you with a program called Medicaid.

So, what are your options for addressing the escalating costs of long-term care? There are five basic options for you to consider.

- Self-insure, or pay for everything out of pocket.
- Purchase long-term care insurance.
- Use specially designed life insurance policies with long-term care features.
- Use specially designed annuities with long-term care features.
- Use some combination of all of the above.

On the next few pages, we will consider each of these options and what you need to know as you consider what is best for you and your family.

Option 1: Self-insure, or pay for everything out of pocket.

That means that you do nothing, and if you someday face a long-term care situation, you will just pay for it out of pocket. For the very, very wealthy, decisions to self-insure may not be a bad risk. However, for most Americans, the prospect of running out of money late in life is a daunting one indeed. If you do not have deep pockets, a decision to self-insure may be risky.

If you do self-insure, and if you later run out of money, the government has another program called Medicaid, which is a program designed for the indigent. Under Medicaid, the government will decide which facility you will be housed in and all the details about how your care will be administered by the government.

Option 2: Purchase long-term care insurance.

This type of insurance is specifically designed to pay for long-term care expenses. Purchasing a long-term care insurance policy can provide powerful protection for your hard-earned assets. It can transfer some or all of the risk of financing long-term care costs to the insurance company. There are about eight million Americans covered by some form of long-term care insurance, according to the 2015 article, "Long-Term-Care Insurance: Is It Worth It?," in the *Wall Street Journal*. But as premiums have risen, sometimes as much as 40 percent a year, fewer and fewer people are seeking this kind of coverage. At the beginning of the last decade, there were one hundred or so companies selling long-term care insurance. Today, there are about a dozen and the number is dwindling.

Option 3: Use specially designed life insurance policies with long-term care features.

If you have accumulated moderate wealth, there are some other options available to you besides long-term care insurance. There are life insurance companies now offering a special type of policy that pays a death benefit just like any other life insurance policy but also has a special long-term care rider that offers some attractive protection against catastrophic long-term health care costs.

In this way, if you live long enough and do not need long-term care, you have the benefit of keeping access to the cash value inside the special life insurance policy.

Option 4: Use specially designed annuities with long-term care features.

In addition to special life insurance policies with long-term care provisions, there are also fixed-rate annuities offered by some insurance companies that are structured in a similar way.

With those, you get the benefit of the annuity during your lifetime, and if you need long-term care, the long-term care benefits built into this special annuity product can be very attractive. If you don't need long-term care, again, like the special life insurance policy, you get to keep your money and the benefits of the annuity, and the long-term care protection comes as a type of bonus.

As you consider your options for protecting yourself and your family from the risks of funding long-term care costs, you should be aware that the pricing for premiums on long-term care insurance are most attractive as you approach your middle fifties. By age sixty, the premiums begin to get much higher at a much faster rate, and by age seventy, they can be virtually unaffordable, no doubt leading to the present difficulties in this segment of the insurance industry.

In my professional practice, we try to have a conversation with our clients about these issues in their early fifties so they can think it through and then act on their decision while they are young enough to get the most attractive pricing.

Hopefully, this discussion of the issues surrounding long-term care has been helpful to you. If you want to learn more, talk to your financial planner or an insurance professional who is knowledgeable about long-term care. Not all of them are, but you can find out pretty quickly just by asking a few key questions.

CHAPTER 16

HOW CAN I HELP OLDER RELATIVES ARTICULATE THEIR LONG-TERM CARE WISHES?

While we are on the topic of preparing for long-term care issues in your own life, let's also discuss the impact of these same issues on aging parents or other relatives.

In the best of all situations, helping an older relative or a parent plan for long-term care and other end-of-life issues happens when they are healthy, and various options can be considered with adequate time to do so. Unfortunately, events can sometimes intervene, and an elderly person's need for assistance can quickly become an emergency.

This possibility of unexpected need is why it is so important for adult children and younger relatives to gather up the courage and preparation to begin a series of important conversations when elderly loved ones are healthy. Once stricken, older relatives may be unable to understand questions or express their wishes in proper detail.

If there is no plan, family members grasp at responsibilities—or shirk them—without any idea of what the older relative would really want. These talks actually should go far beyond money.

There should be discussions about independence and basic preferences for the way the individual wants to live or die.

Demographers believe that with the rising number of single Americans—those divorced or never married—these conversations will become increasingly complicated, as they fall to nieces and nephews, younger friends, or designated representatives. Want to avoid a worst-case scenario? *Start the conversation now.* Here are some ideas:

1. Start with the most important priorities.

Maybe this first conversation isn't just about where the will or health care power of attorney is, though you will eventually have to get to that. Maybe this conversation is about you noticing that a parent or loved one is moving more slowly, is more forgetful, is clearly looking like their health has taken a turn for the worse— and maybe that is why you want to know where the will is. *Jumping into money issues first is usually a mistake.* Consider dealing with immediate health and lifestyle issues first.

2. Prepare your questions in advance.

When a parent or relative is unconscious or unresponsive, the younger relative is immediately in the driver's seat. That is why it is critical to make a list of questions for the elderly relative to answer in detail while they have the capacity to address them.

What You Need to Know

When you discuss long-term care with an older relative, try to focus on the purpose of the conversation, rather than the distracting emotional issues that are likely to pop up. Remember, you need some basic information. Here is a simple checklist:

- Where are the important papers?
- How are household expenses paid?
- Who are the doctors and specialists?
- What medicines are being taken?
- Is there a will, an advanced directive, and a funeral plan?
- If there is a funeral plan, what money or burial insurance is designated to pay for it?

There may be dozens more questions beyond these, based on your family's personal circumstances. But in creating this list, ask yourself: "What do I need to know if my family member suddenly becomes sick or dies?"

3. Turn the conversation to affording long-term care.

One of the greatest continuing fallacies about long-term care is that Medicare pays for it—Medicare pays for a significant amount of medical care *associated* with long-term care, but it does not pay for the actual cost of home-based or nursing home-based care.

Private-room nursing home care costs can run in the $50,000 to 70,000 range per year. That is a lot for anyone's budget. As we have already discussed, long-term care insurance is something that should be purchased in your fifties for the best chance at affordability, so the conversation needs to be a mixture of preferences and finances. If an elderly person cannot afford top-quality care, families need to plan alternatives, especially if it means pitching in.

4. Be patient.

In some families, having a successful financial discussion means several attempts and some frustration. Try not to become angry or frustrated if this happens. Just keep starting the conversation until it catches on. It might make sense to say something like, "You've always been so independent, Mom. I just want you to give us the right instructions so we do exactly what you want."

5. Offer to get some qualified advice.

If you do not fully understand your relative's financial affairs, it might make sense for you both to talk to an attorney, a tax professional, a financial advisor, or some combination of all three.

A qualified advisor can help you straighten out whatever confusion exists, can help you put specific legal documents in place, and can set up ways to pay medical and household bills if your loved one becomes unable to do so. If you can, involve your priest, preacher, or church elder in that conversation—an impartial third party can sometimes move things along.

The Three Essentials

Above all, an aging relative should have, at a minimum, these three things:
- a current will
- a durable power of attorney
- a health care power of attorney

Have these documents in place and easily accessible. Actually, just creating or reviewing those documents can be a good starting point for making sure other necessary plans are in place. More on estate-planning later in this book.

6. Plan a care-giving strategy together.

You should discuss the relative's preferences and trigger points for various stages of health care.

Most people will almost always want to stay at home, but you should have an honest discussion about how much you can do at home as a caregiver and whether various services (home health aide, geriatric care manager, assisted living) should be introduced at various stages. Talking through what a parent will be able to live with at various health stages and putting that information in writing will save plenty of doubt and bitterness later.

7. Discuss what should happen with the home.

If an elderly relative becomes sick and irreversibly incapacitated, the equity in the home may come under consideration as a resource to pay uncovered medical or household maintenance. Since the home is both a major asset and an emotional focal point, it is best to get good advice and spell out specifically what the elderly relative wants done with his property and under what conditions.

8. Make sure everyone knows the plan.

Once you settle on a strategy, make sure all family and friends understand the plan and their assignments.

It can take a lot of time, emotional energy, and lots of love to have these important health care conversations. It may be a challenge to make the conversations happen, but if you can do it while your loved ones are still healthy, it will make it so much easier for you and other members of your family if and when the time comes for dealing with long-term care issues.

FROM OUR FILES...

Revealing Conversations

The kinds of conversations we have discussed in this chapter can yield surprising results, including some experiences that will linger long in the memory.

Take the hypothetical case of Jim and Judy, who were referred to a qualified financial advisor. Jim was a general practitioner doctor in a small town. As the advisor met with them for the first time, their story began to unfold like a bad nightmare.

Out of the blue, Jim had suffered a major stroke and had been in the hospital for about a week in a coma-like state. Judy had been at his bedside for most of that time and was, among other things, coming to grips with the idea that she might lose her husband. Judy began to realize that Jim had always handled family financial matters and she had very little knowledge of what they had or where they had it. She had no idea how she was going to take care of herself if something happened to Jim.

Fortunately, Jim snapped out of it, remarkably with little apparent effects from the stroke. This amazing outcome gave Jim and Judy the opportunity to discuss their personal financial affairs, really for the first time in their married life. As they talked, Judy began to understand all the work Jim had done to make sure Judy would be well taken care of if something were to happen to him prematurely. They both realized they needed to get their affairs in order and get Judy up to speed with the knowledge and skills to carry on in Jim's absence.

But before they could actually get much done or put a plan in writing, Jim suffered a second stroke. The outcome was very much like the first one. Jim was in the hospital, unable to communicate, in a coma-like state. Judy was back in the position she had been in just a few weeks earlier. She knew very little and was fearful about her future.

Like a miracle of mercy from heaven, Jim once again snapped out of it and once again showed little or no damage from the stroke. It was at this point that the financial advisor got the call to set up a meeting with Jim and Judy. The advisor talked with them about what was important to them, about their goals and dreams for the future, and about their intentions to care for their children. The advisor stressed the importance of having a well-thought-out financial plan and a systematic, step-by-step process to achieve each of their goals and intentions. The advisor explained that having a clear plan and taking the proper steps to make that plan a reality would eventually lead to peace of mind about financial matters. They agreed and embarked on a journey that eventually led to getting everything in place, getting every element of their plan addressed, and placing clearly on the horizon every one of their goals.

Many months later, everything was in order, all the necessary documents in place, and Judy was much more knowledgeable and confident than ever before. At a follow-up review meeting, it became clear that there were no more issues to address—no more stones to turn. Judy's eyes began to tear up and she said to her advisor, "I am so grateful we found you and for all you have done." Jim stood up, gave the advisor a firm, two-handed handshake, looked him in the eye, and said he couldn't thank me enough for all I had done for Judy and him.

That was the last time the advisor ever saw Jim. One week later, he died quietly at his home.

A few hours after Jim's funeral, Judy told her advisor she knew that everything was handled and because of that, she was able to focus on being with her children and the rest of the family and honoring Jim's memory. She said, "Not once since the moment Jim died did I even think about financial matters or how I was going to take care of myself."

The peace of mind that she felt was immeasurable. Judy confided that when their advisor first met with them, she had no idea what financial peace of mind meant. She realized that at the time, she really had no frame of reference to even understand the concept. Judy went on to say, "Now I get it about financial peace of mind and how valuable it can be. If you ever have someone that doesn't get it, you have them call me and I will explain it to them!"

This story captures everything about the value of taking the time to get clear about what is important in your life—and then creating a definite plan to make it happen.

Is financial peace of mind achievable? Of course it is possible. How valuable is it? Ask Judy. She will tell you!

FINANCE 102:
Common Scenario Planning

II. PLANNING FOR GROWTH AND PROSPERITY

In the first part of the book, we talked about the ways in which you can intelligently increase your wealth while moderating your risks. That, in a nutshell, is what the art of investing is all about.

To master this, or any other art, you must, of course, first understand it. Not everybody pauses to do that.

CHAPTER 17

WHAT'S THE DIFFERENCE BETWEEN GROWTH- AND INCOME- ORIENTED INVESTMENTS?

Do you ever feel confused by investments? Have you ever wondered why one particular investment behaves so differently than another investment?

Well, there certainly are many different kinds of investments to choose from. And each of these choices opens up many other choices. It can get confusing and maybe even overwhelming in a hurry.

For example, if we look at stocks, there are thousands and thousands to choose from. There are stocks of large companies, small companies, and all sizes in-between. There are US stocks and stocks of companies headquartered outside the United States. Do you know which stocks are right for you? Or maybe a bond is better. But if we look at bonds, again there are thousands to choose from, and there are several different types available. There are US government bonds, corporate bonds, and bonds issued by state or city governments. There are bonds issued by foreign governments and foreign corporations. This list goes on and on. Which of these should be in your portfolio? Again, all this is potentially very confusing. Take these steps to better understand the landscape:

1. Reduce all the possibilities to two.

If you were to look at all the investment possibilities out there, put all of them in a great big pot, and boil them down to their most basic essence, what you would find is that there are really only two broad categories of investments: investments that seek to grow over time and investments that don't grow but which produce income.

A Universe of Two

1. Growth: There are investments that have the potential to grow in value over time.
2. Income: There are investments that tend to produce income but really don't grow very much over time.

In other words, there are growth-oriented investments, and there are income-oriented investments. Now two broad categories seem a little more manageable than thousands of choices, wouldn't you agree?

2. Consider how growth investments and income investments project over time.

Time and money. If we were to look at the historical performance of asset classes that are classified as "growth investments," what we may find is that they historically increased in value over a long period of time.

The following graph is a simple illustration of the long term goal of an asset classified as a growth investment, versus the long term goal of an asset classified as an income oriented investment. As you can see, the growth investment curve looks almost like a

45-degree angle, headed up like a jet taking off. Now, if we look at the curve of income-oriented investments, we see the value increase is much less exciting and, over time, really doesn't do too much to help our money grow. (See Fig. 1)

Growth and Income *Fig. 1*

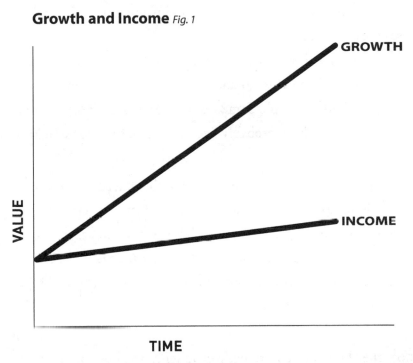

An illustration of long term goals of Growth oriented investments and Income oriented investments. This is for illustrative purposes only and is not actual performance. Results will vary. Past performance doesn't guarantee future results.

Now, if investments acted exactly like this graph, everybody would make a lot of money, and investment professionals like me would be out of a job. So, there is probably a catch. Well, the catch here is that this graph is an illustration of investing goals, and not an actual performance. In addition, to help meet investment goals, a long term commitment may be required.

Let's take a look at a different graph that takes into account a long time horizon.

The graph on the next page (See Fig. 2) is an illustration of the route an investor may encounter through the course of their investing career. The stock market goes up and down. Real estate prices go up and down. Gold prices go up and down. That which rises must eventually fall.

Volatility. Anything that can grow in value will likely fluctuate in price over time. This up-and-down price movement is called "volatility." Some people compare the ups and downs to a roller coaster ride. You have probably been on a roller coaster sometime in your life, haven't you?

Most people would agree that when the roller coaster is going up, it is pretty exciting. But when the roller coaster is headed down, the stomach starts moving closer to the throat, and at the steepest part of that downward slide, some people will begin to make vague promises like, "Help! If you'll get me off this thing, I promise I won't do this again!"

Some people think this roller coaster analogy fits very well for how they how they emotionally experience the ups and downs of investing.

Growth and Income *Fig. 2*

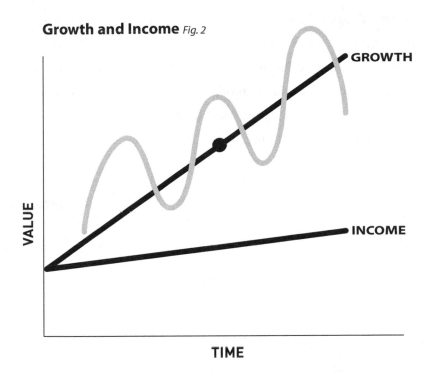

An illustration of long term goals of Growth oriented investments and Income oriented investments. This is for illustrative purposes only and is not actual performance. Results will vary. Past performance doesn't guarantee future results.

Investing over time. One important thing to remember about growth oriented investments is that while they have the potential to grow over time, investors will experience many ups and downs along the way, in addition to the potential of losing value. Now, if we take a look at the income side of things, we find that income-oriented investments do not tend to cause near the "tummy" trouble that growth investments do. It is the difference between a train ride and a roller coaster ride—between Amtrak and the Coney Island Cyclone. So when I say "income-oriented investments," what I am talking about would include certificates of deposit, Treasury bills, Treasury bonds, corporate bonds, and so on. Sure, income investments do move up and down from time to time, but the amount of up and down movement is usually not enough to cause too much emotional upset, especially compared to growth oriented investments. However, income investments don't produce much gain over time. *(See Fig. 3)*

Growth and Income *Fig. 3*

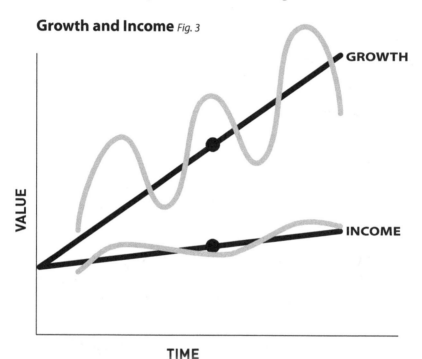

An illustration of long term goals of Growth oriented investments and Income oriented investments. This is for illustrative purposes only and is not actual performance. Results will vary. Past performance doesn't guarantee future results.

Balanced investment portfolio. Most people eventually find that they cannot afford to keep all of their investments only in income-oriented investments, and most people wouldn't sleep well at night if they had all of their money allocated to growth investments. What happens for most people is they end up with a mix of investments.

(See Fig. 4) They find the right balance of growth vs. income investments that will help them achieve their long-term financial goals and still allow them to sleep well at night. Finding this right balance, this right ratio, if you will, is a process called "asset allocation." While it doesn't guarantee returns or protect against a loss, the right asset allocation—the right balance for *you*—is critical to your long-term success.

Growth and Income *Fig. 4*

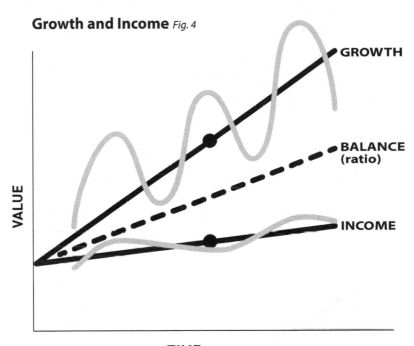

An illustration of long term goals of Growth oriented investments and Income oriented investments. This is for illustrative purposes only and is not actual performance. Results will vary. Past performance doesn't guarantee future results.

To help you find that perfect balance, it is important to understand the growth roller coaster and what its characteristic up-and-down behavior really means over time. If we look at growth investments over time and look at any given year over the past nearly nine decades, the range of possibility on whether you made money or lost money—well the range is enormous. *(See Fig. 5)* In any given year, almost anything could happen (and most anything you can think of *has* happened over time).

Time may level the steep drops. However, if we choose any given year and then look at the next rolling five years, we may find that the roller coaster may flatten out quite a bit. For example, if we were to examine the history of the S&P 500, we can see that in most rolling five-year time periods, the S&P 500 gained in value more often than not. The roller coaster almost completely flattens out when we look at ten-year rolling time periods. By the time we look at twenty-year rolling time periods, there is virtually no period the S&P 500 lost value. While past performance doesn't guarantee future results, the history of the S&P 500 Index suggests that volatility flattens out over longer periods of time.

Reducing Risk Over Time *Fig. 5*

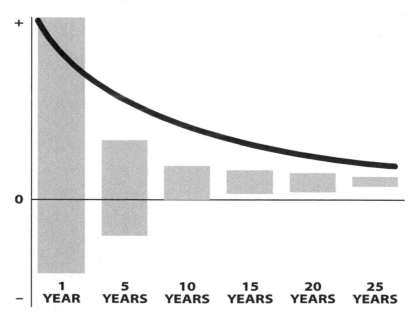

The key message here is the importance of time and how it affects the long-term performance of investments—especially growth investments. Many of us may need to have some growth investments in order to help reach our long-term goals and stay ahead of inflation. We need to allow enough time to help meet our investment objectives with growth oriented investments. Consider the up-and-down roller coaster to be a natural part of the process if we keep the time factor in mind.

Also, keep in mind that what I have shown you here is past history over a long period of time. In the investment world, we always have to remind people, "Past performance is no guarantee of future results." That said, I have found in my investment career that studying how things have worked in the past can be very helpful in shaping how to think about the future.

Hopefully, you are now armed with a little more investment knowledge than you had before and are better positioned to make more logical choices about your own investments.

Now, let's look at some of the investment options and "vehicles" (or "products," like stocks, etc.) available to you

CHAPTER 18

HOW DO I NARROW MY INVESTMENT OPTIONS?

When it comes to investing, you have a wide variety of approaches and investment vehicles to choose from. Narrowing down those choices is sometimes a matter of personal preference, convenience, or cost. Let's review some of the most popular investment vehicles available to you.

Individual securities.

The first option is individual securities—generally, stocks and bonds. If you buy stock, you are *purchasing shares* of a particular company. If you buy a bond—whether it is a Treasury bond, a corporate bond, or even a municipal bond—you are *lending money* at a stated rate of interest for a particular period of time.

Whenever you buy or sell an individual security, you are typically charged a *transaction fee*. As a result, anyone who assembles and maintains a well-diversified portfolio of securities can run up a sizeable tab in transaction costs.

Mutual funds.

An alternative to a portfolio of individual securities is a mutual fund—usually, a collection of securities selected and managed by a professional. When you select a mutual fund, you *purchase a share in a diversified portfolio of securities* in a single transaction.

In addition, you receive the potential benefit of professional security selection, supervision, and management of that portfolio. Of course, these benefits do come at a cost. As a result, you will pay *management fees and expenses* in connection with your mutual fund investments. We will return to a discussion of mutual funds later in this chapter.

Exchange-traded funds.

Another option is an exchange-traded fund or ETF. Like mutual funds, ETFs let you buy a share of a portfolio of securities in a single transaction. However, unlike mutual funds, ETFs are traded on an exchange, just like stocks. Typically, internal management fees and expenses in ETFs are substantially lower than in traditional mutual funds. Many investors find ETFs an attractive, low-cost alternative to mutual funds. In addition, ETFs are sometimes considered an attractive alternative to purchasing individual securities.

Please keep in mind that ETFs will fluctuate with changes in market conditions and are not suitable for all investors. In many cases, ETFs have lower expense ratios than comparable index funds. However, since ETFs trade like stocks, they are subject to brokerage fees and trading spreads. Therefore, ETFs are not effective for dollar cost averaging small amounts over time, and likewise any strategy using ETFs must account for these additional costs. ETFs do not necessarily trade at the net asset values of their underlying holdings, meaning an ETF could potentially trade above or below the value of the underlying portfolio.

Individual securities, mutual funds, and exchange-traded funds each represent advantages and disadvantages for investors. Choosing the right mix can be a challenge. We will continue to examine these methods—and other considerations you should be aware of as you make decisions about how to invest your money.

CHAPTER 19

WHAT'S A MUNICIPAL BOND, AND HOW DO I CHOOSE ONE WISELY?

Municipal bonds have long been a safe haven for higher-income investors looking for greater safety and greater tax efficiency. So, what is a municipal bond? Let's start with a definition. A municipal bond, or muni, is a bond issued by a state or local government or its agencies to raise funds for a host of reasons tied to keeping the government going and serving needs in the community.

The potential issuers may include cities, counties, redevelopment agencies, water and sewer projects, school districts, publicly owned airports, seaports, and other transportation entities. The proceeds from the sale of bonds pay for everything from immediate government expenses to new roads and various public projects.

MUNICIPAL BONDS

Municipal bonds come in two flavors—general obligation bonds and revenue bonds.

- **General obligation bonds** are intended to raise immediate capital to cover government expenses.
- **Revenue bonds** are the ones that fund infrastructure projects.

As an incentive for investors to buy these bonds, interest income is often exempt from federal income tax as well as the income tax of the state in which they are issued.

Mutual funds that invest in municipal bonds also offer the same tax treatment as if you owned municipal bonds directly, that is, they are typically exempt from federal income tax as well as the income tax of the state in which they are issued. Generally, one of the best sources of demand for municipal bonds is the individual investor. Besides the tax-free income, another attraction for investors is safety. *There is a very low default rate associated with municipal bonds*, which means muni investors almost always get their money back in the end, and their interest payments along the way. For example, even during the Great Depression, no state defaulted on its general-obligation bonds, and while some municipal bonds have defaulted, overall, such defaults are rare. So where is the opportunity for you?

Look at the tax-free income yields available in municipal bonds. You may find some attractive net after-tax yields that you probably wouldn't find in Certificates of Deposit, Treasury securities, and some other investments.

FOUR BOND-BUYING TIPS TO KNOW

Before you buy, here are four important things to know and steps to follow.

1. Find out if municipal bonds are right for you.

The first call you make should not be to a bond broker. It should be to your tax professional to be clear about your tax bracket and how a stream of tax-free income would benefit your overall income tax picture. Once you know that, *then* talk with your financial advisor.

Make sure you are seeing the big picture. Have your advisor take a look at your entire taxable investment portfolio, and determine whether or not investing in municipal bonds is the right approach to take for your investments. Also, keep in mind that there is no point in putting tax-exempt municipal bonds into tax-exempt accounts like IRAs or 401(k) plans. These types of retirement accounts are tax advantaged already, and there will be no benefit for using tax-exempt bonds inside of tax-deferred accounts. In fact, there might even be a penalty.

Your financial advisor can explain this in more detail.

2. Keep an eye peeled for the AMT.

While most municipal bonds pay interest that is free from federal income taxes, some may pay rates that are subject to the alternative minimum tax, known as the AMT. It is a little more complicated than we have room for here, but the *alternative minimum tax* and its impact on tax-free municipal bonds is important to know and understand. Be sure to talk with your tax professional or financial planner before making a move into municipal bonds.

3. Don't forget to ladder.

"Laddering" is a portfolio structuring term. To ladder bonds means that you are buying them with maturities occurring at regular intervals, so when they mature, you will have money to reinvest at those same regular intervals. Following this "laddering" portfolio structure can help stabilize the impact of changing interest rates on your investment portfolio.

4. Watch those safety ratings.

Yes, the main private investment ratings firms—Moody's and Standard & Poor's among them—have been in the doghouse for rating many battered investments highly, not just municipal bonds. Still, most municipals rated AA or AAA are generally safe to consider. It is also important to check the issuer's long-term ratings history. If they have been consistently highly ranked over decades and the municipality has no financial scandal (something that can be checked through news archives on the Internet), that is another good way to research a bond issuer before making a purchase.

Tax-free municipal bonds can be a great alternative to other income investments and can provide a high degree of safety for your income-oriented investments. If you are in a higher income tax bracket, the tax-free income available from municipal bonds may actually exceed the income available from other income investment alternatives on a net, after tax basis.

Just take your time, get professional advice, and make wise picks of the best to add to your portfolio.

CHAPTER 20

HOW DO I APPROPRIATELY ALLOCATE MY ASSETS?

Here is some advice you have heard a million times: "Don't put all your eggs in one basket." Before you shrug off this seemingly trite adage, pause for a moment to reflect on how much truth is in it. This actually is rather sage advice, especially important when it comes to investments. The question then becomes how many of which eggs need to be in which basket?

In the investment world, your hard-earned assets are the eggs, and the various asset classes available to you are the baskets. The important process of deciding how much to invest in which asset class is called "asset allocation."

Many academic studies have been published on the topic of asset allocation. Over and over again, they have concluded that asset allocation is one of the most critical factors in the investment process. One example of this type of research often cited by many investment professionals is "Determinants of Portfolio Performance", by Gary P Brinson, L. Randolph Hood, and Gilbert L. Beebower, published in the July/August 1986 Financial Analysts Journal which led the authors to conclude that asset allocation explained 93.6% of the variation in a portfolio's returns.

Other factors, such as security selection and market timing, are less critical and have much less impact on the overall long-term performance picture. They are still important, just less so than most people would think.

When designing your own personal investment picture, you should *pay particular attention to how much you invest in which kind of asset and why*. Take time to understand the significance of your asset allocation decisions.

In dealing with investments, you may find it helpful to seek professional help. Talk to a CERTIFIED FINANCIAL PLANNER™ professional or other knowledgeable investment professional to make sure that your investment portfolio's asset allocation is appropriate for your needs. Do not go with a hunch. And about those eggs? Well, you know what not to do. So just don't. In the long run, you may be glad you paid attention to this tip!

FROM OUR FILES...

The Eggs in Ralph's Basket

"Don't put all your eggs in one basket." It is advice we have all heard many times before, and we all know it is true. If that one basket falls, you lose all the eggs, right? But if this piece of advice is distilled wisdom, like many other old adages we hear, then why don't we follow the advice?

In the investment world, we talk about the importance of "diversification." Diversification is just a fancier term for the same not-all-eggs-in-one-basket concept.

Take the hypothetical story of an investor named Ralph. Ralph was a successful businessman with a growing retirement account. His accountant got involved in a "hot" new investment and offered to "let" Ralph in on the deal. This investment was so good that it was worth "betting the farm" on it because it was such a "sure thing," as his accountant excitedly told him. Sadly, Ralph bought into the idea and chose to invest all of his retirement funds in this "once in a lifetime opportunity." All he needed to do, he was assured, was to sit back and wait for the money to roll in. Visions of an early retirement floated through Ralph's head.

Unfortunately, what actually happened was that the business activity of the investment was really a front for selling and transporting illegal drugs. The US Drug Enforcement Administration seized all the assets of the operation, all the people involved went to jail or were killed, and the investors lost all of their investment. Ralph's retirement savings disappeared almost overnight.

Lack of diversification can be expensive.

Here is another example. An investor named Peter owned a large quantity of a "blue chip" stock and enjoyed a very healthy dividend flow that financed his very comfortable lifestyle. Peter's financial advisor repeatedly counseled him over many years about the risk of having way too much of his total net worth tied up in one single stock.

Peter tried to reassure his financial advisor that he was fine because the company issuing the "blue-chip stock" was such a fine company and was so large and so well established, that, well, there just wasn't really any risk to it. That was until the fall of 2008 when the financial world in the United States began to fall apart and did so rapidly.

This particular stock Peter held had once been the darling of Wall Street and always made the top of the list of the highest dividend-paying stocks of any "blue-chip" company. Suddenly, the company issuing Peter's stocks was teetering on the edge of serious financial difficulties. The stock plummeted in value and very soon after, the company announced that it was cutting its dividend to one cent per share. Overnight, Peter's stock, once a safe bet for anybody's portfolio, became one of the lowest dividend-paying stocks in the country.

Peter had his income cut dramatically, basically overnight. His net worth fell by a large factor, and he never recovered. This hypothetical investor, Peter, is a "poster child" of why diversification is important.

The lesson here is that no matter how good the story is, no matter how much you believe things will work out, there is always risk that things may change. Do not take the risk. Always diversify your assets. That way, if there is a bad situation, it will only affect a small portion of what you have worked so hard to save.

THE MAGIC WORD IS "DIVERSIFICATION"

"Don't put all your eggs in one basket" is advice so vital to the health of your investment portfolio, I want to spend a little more time discussing it. The fact is, if you have too large a portion of your total investment assets invested in any one security or type of security, you may experience problems at some point down the road. Murphy's Law tells us that, "Anything that can go wrong probably will." When it comes to investments, Murphy certainly knew what he was talking about.

No matter how good and solid an investment opportunity might appear to be, there is always the possibility that something can—and sometimes will—go wrong.

Talk to a long-time Enron employee whose retirement portfolio consisted mostly of company stock that collapsed in late 2001. Ask them about how it feels to be totally wiped out overnight, to see their plans for a comfortable retirement evaporate before their eyes.

Diversification, while it does not guarantee investment returns or protect against a loss, is a powerful investment tool that can help protect you from concentrating too much risk in any single security or class of investments. When we assemble an investment portfolio for a client, we diversify their asset allocation so there is no concentration of risk anywhere in their portfolio. In addition to analyzing accounts and investments individually, we look at the client's overall portfolio in an "x-ray" view to determine if there is some hidden concentration of risk lurking somewhere that is not obvious.

The bottom line is simply this: Whenever someone tells you to put all your money into any one investment or type of investment, there is only one correct response. Run quickly in the other direction.

THE IMPORTANCE OF INTERNATIONAL DIVERSIFICATION

There was a time when many American investors only considered investing in the United States. And there was a time when that might have been okay. It wasn't so long ago that the United States was the lion's share of where one could invest money around the world. But today, the US makes up only about half of the world's financial markets.

If you only invest in the US, you are leaving about half of the world's investment opportunity out of your investment picture. In today's world, leaving nearly two-thirds of the world's available opportunity out of your investment strategy just may not make sense. So, how much should you have in international investments?

To find the right amount of international investments to fit in your personal portfolio, you may need to consult with a CERTIFIED FINANCIAL PLANNER™ professional or other qualified investment adviser representative. Also, you should know that investing internationally has unique risks that are different than investing solely in the United States.

For example, there might be *political risk* or *currency risk*. These are not the same things. Governments might experience disruptions; currencies might change in value relative to the US dollar. These factors might affect the performance of your international investments. Additional risks are lower liquidity, economic risks, and different accounting methodologies. Carefully monitored and managed, these risks may be lessened or even be made to work in your favor.

When investing overseas, do not forget one of the basic tenets of successful investing—to broadly diversify your investments. Remember the advice to not put all your eggs in one basket. (Okay. That's the last time I'll use that phrase in this book. But remember it anyway!)

Consider investments in well-developed countries as well as countries whose economies are part of the world's emerging markets. A well-diversified portfolio of domestic and international investments may help position you to make money wherever in the world there is money to be made.

CHAPTER 21

SHOULD I TAKE AN ACTIVE OR PASSIVE APPROACH TO MANAGING MY PORTFOLIO?

There are many investment theories on Wall Street. Virtually all of them have some value at some point in time—depending on market conditions. One ongoing debate among investors is the advantages and disadvantages of a "buy and hold" versus an "active" investment strategy.

Both strategies start with the selection of quality securities that the investment manager believes will perform well over time. This, however, is where the similarities end. Simply put, the buy-and-hold or passive manager keeps those securities regardless of what the markets do or how the returns fluctuate over time, while an active-investment manager will continually monitor each security carefully over time. If a particular security is not performing as expected, it may be sold and replaced with a new security that appears to offer better prospects going forward.

An active-investment manager might also sell certain securities and buy others to "rebalance" the overall portfolio to stay in line with predetermined asset allocation targets.

This practice of constantly monitoring the performance of securities and the periodic rebalancing of portfolios that is characteristic of an active management strategy will sometimes result in more short-term gains or losses than might be experienced with a long-term buy-and-hold strategy.

So which is better—buy and hold or active management?

To answer that question, you should consider the overall bottom-line performance over time. If, on an after-tax net bottom-line basis, you made more money with one strategy versus the other, the best choice is probably the strategy that gives you the best performance. My personal preference is an active-management approach to handling investments because it provides greater flexibility. Investment conditions are constantly changing, and active management provides the flexibility to adapt to changing market conditions as they evolve.

There are always investment opportunities, no matter what the current market conditions, and active management provides the flexibility to move when it is time to move and to capitalize on opportunities as they happen. If you have been a buy-and-hold investor, you may want to consider taking a second look at the advantages of a more active-management strategy for your investments.

And take the time to inform yourself about how well your investments are doing—by looking more closely at the numbers to see what matters most: the real rate of return on your money.

CHAPTER 22

WHAT'S MY REAL RATE OF RETURN?

How do you know what your investments are earning? It is important to know and to understand the factors that affect your true bottom line. That is your real rate of return.

For example, let us suppose that you bought a certificate of deposit at your local bank that pays 3 percent interest. You might assume that your capital is increasing at 3 percent per year. Unfortunately, that is not necessarily the case. To realistically evaluate the earnings on your CD, you must calculate the real rate of return of that investment.

THE REAL RATE OF RETURN

To know your real rate of return, you need to consider three factors:
- the nominal return on your investment
- the impact the current rate of inflation will have on the purchasing power of your earnings
- the income tax that will be due on your earnings

Let's say the nominal rate of return on your CD is 3 percent, but let's suppose that inflation is running at 2 percent per year, so the purchasing power of your earnings will be reduced by that amount. If you are in the 33 percent tax bracket for federal income tax purposes, then one-third of your earnings, or 1 percent, will be paid out in taxes.

For the purposes of our example, we will leave state income taxes out of the picture, but if you have a state income tax, you should also deduct that amount from the nominal rate. So, let's now calculate the real rate of return on our 3 percent CD. *In this case, your hypothetical CD is actually earning a real rate of return of zero percent.*

> **Nominal return on CD 3%**
> **Less inflation rate -2%**
> **Less income taxes -1%**
> **Net Real Rate of Return 0%**

You thought you were getting a safe, secure return of 3 percent. The reality, however, is that you actually end up with nothing when you factor how inflation impacts the purchasing power of your earnings and the tax hit you will take on those earnings.

Rate of return on muni bonds. To further illustrate this real rate of return concept, let's take a look at another type of investment, tax-free municipal bonds. For the purposes of illustration, let's look at a hypothetical municipal bond paying 4 percent.

As before, we take the nominal rate of return (4 percent) and subtract the inflation factor (2 percent). There are no tax consequences to factor, since in this case, there are no federal income taxes on the municipal bond. Therefore, our net real rate of return is 2 percent.

> Nominal return on muni bond 4%
> Less inflation rate -2%
> Less income taxes -0%
> Net Real Rate of Return 2%

Rate of return on securities. Let's look at one more example. This time we add a small layer of complexity. Let's suppose you own a blue-chip stock that earned a 12 percent total return this year. The total return in this case was made up of 8 percent capital appreciation and 4 percent dividend income.

To keep the example as simple as possible, let's suppose we sold the stock and realized a long-term gain on the sale. The inflation rate remains at 2 percent. The current tax rate for both dividends and capital gains for many taxpayers is 15 percent of earnings, or 1.8 percent. If you do the math, you will find that you earned a net return of 8.2 percent.

> Nominal return on stock 12%
> (8% appreciation, 4% dividends)
> Less inflation rate -2%
> Less income taxes -1.8%
> Net Real Rate of Return 8.2%

So now you know how to quickly analyze the real rate of return on your investments. Remember, you just take the nominal rate of return, subtract the current inflation rate, and then deduct all the income taxes that would be due based on current tax laws. By making this simple calculation, you will better analyze and compare different investments, improve your investment decisions, and know where you stand with your investments—and you'll have peace of mind because there will be no unpleasant surprises.

CHAPTER 23

HOW CAN I WIN WITH MY INVESTMENTS OVER TIME?

When financial markets are rising, it is easy to be excited about how much money you are making. The exhilaration of seeing your investment accounts swell in value can be very heady indeed. On the other hand, watching your account balances fall can be very depressing—and may even cause significant stress. If you are going to have investments, you really ought to consider the impact of capital preservation math. What is capital preservation math? Why is it important? Just because it is "math," don't skip this useful piece of investment-related information.

THE THREE LAWS OF CAPITAL PRESERVATION MATH

There are three laws to remember if you want to understand the impact of capital preservation math.

The first law: Gains are easier to lose than they are to make.

You probably sensed this anyway, but here is how it works: if you invested $1,000 and it grew over time to $1,500, then you would have a 50 percent gain.

That part is easy and exciting, and if all you had was steady growth, you could stop right here. But, remember, investments go up as well as down, and if your $1,500 investment then falls to $1,000 in value, you have just lost 33 percent of your investment value. In other words, *it only takes a 33 percent loss to fully wipe out a 50 percent gain.* So, law number one for capital preservation math—gains are easier to lose than they are to make.

Capital Preservation Math

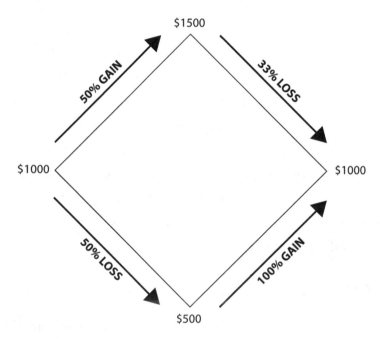

The second law: Losses are hard to overcome.

Here is another example. Suppose we took that same $1,000 investment but, over time, the value of that investment fell to $500. We have lost 50 percent of our investment. And, worse, to make it up, we will now have to make a 100 percent gain on our investment just to get back to where we started. *It will take a 100 percent gain to make up for a 50 percent loss.* So, law number two for capital preservation math—losses are hard to overcome.

The third law: Mitigating large losses can help improve performance over time.

Based on researching investment performance over long periods of time, the general return pattern that helps us win over the long term is that we need to do two simple things:

A. Outperform in weak markets.

B. Keep up in strong markets.

Over longer periods of time, this lets capital preservation math work in our favor. For example, let us look at one of the most difficult market periods in recent history. In the fall of 2008, we had a market meltdown of major proportions. Just about every investment category lost money, and this gloomy dark financial cloud spread all over the world. Lots of people lost lots of money in the fall of 2008.

In fact, many people began to talk of the 2002–2012 period as a "lost decade" because of how the decade had performed overall, how bad the losses were in 2008, and how painful recovery has been. And yet, suppose we owned an investment that had only done "okay" during this ten-year time period.

This investment would have slightly underperformed its benchmark or maybe just kept up in each of the years from 2002 to 2012—*except* in 2008. In 2008, this investment lost some value, like most everything else at the time, but it lost substantially less than most.

This is an example of an investment that *outperformed in weak markets*, meaning it lost less than other similar investments at the time, and just *kept up in stronger markets*. In our example, the end result would be that the ten-year performance would actually likely exceed a benchmark index, even though we slightly underperformed or just kept up with the benchmark nine out of the ten years. Losing less, or not losing at all, is the key to understanding and benefiting from capital preservation math.

This is an important point in thinking about investing in general: we do not have to make big, spectacular returns on our investments to win over the long term. We do not even have to outperform every benchmark every year! We just need to make sure we are *well-diversified* and adequately protected from a downturn so that we either do not lose, or we do not lose as much, in falling markets.

THE GENIUS OF THE TORTOISE

Slow and steady positive returns, coupled with little or no losses along the way, will win every time. Chasing after the big win and taking excessive risks has the potential to hurt you in the long run.

REMEMBER THE THREE LAWS OF CAPITAL PRESERVATION MATH.

Law number 1: Gains are easier to lose than they are to make.
Law number 2: Losses are hard to overcome.
Law number 3: Mitigating large losses can help provide outperformance over time.

CHAPTER 24

WHAT TYPES OF MUTUAL
FUNDS SHOULD I BUY?

For many investors, mutual funds have become a popular way to build a well-diversified portfolio and have the potential benefit of active professional management. They are the most common investment vehicles found in most retirement plans offered by employers across America.

There are literally thousands of mutual funds available to choose from, so deciding which ones to buy can be a challenge. But armed with some basic information and an understanding of the different fund categories available, you can be in a better position to develop your investment strategy and asset allocation using mutual funds to build your portfolio. Here are some lists that I think you will find helpful.

THE FIVE VARIETIES OF EQUITY MUTUAL FUNDS

Equity mutual funds can be broadly divided into the five large categories listed below. These large groupings are often referred to as *domestic equity funds* for exclusively US stock investments, *international equity funds* for stock investments outside the United States, and *global equity funds* for stock investments anywhere on the planet.

1. Aggressive growth funds are among the riskiest equity funds. Aimed at maximum capital appreciation, the managers of these funds invest in companies with the potential for rapid growth. Aggressive growth funds may tend to favor smaller, fast-growing companies. Look at our investment pyramid, and you will see where this fund might fit into your plans.

2. Growth funds also strive for capital appreciation, and do so by investing in companies positioned for strong earnings growth. In general, they are slightly less risky than aggressive growth funds. Growth funds may tend to favor larger, more well-established companies with good potential for growth, but probably not as fast as the growth one might expect from aggressive growth funds. The reason is that large companies tend to grow more slowly than smaller companies.

3. Growth and income funds attempt to provide both dividend income and capital appreciation. This category often invests in larger, well-established companies with good dividend-paying capabilities and sometimes may include some bonds in the portfolio as well.

4. Balanced funds offer one-stop shopping by combining stocks and bonds in a single portfolio.

5. Sector funds concentrate on one industry such as technology, financial, health care, or natural resources. Or a sector fund might focus on certain commodities, such as gold, natural gas, oil, or copper.

THE FOUR FIXED-INCOME CATEGORIES OF MUTUAL FUNDS

Bond funds can also be divided into broad categories. There are four types you might want to consider: tax-exempt, taxable, high-yield, and money market funds. (As with mutual funds, there are also international and global versions of these bond funds.) And remember to calculate the real rate of return.

1. Tax-exempt funds buy bonds issued by state and municipal agencies in the United States. Generally, for US taxpayers, these bonds are exempt from federal income taxes and may be exempt from state income taxes, as well.

2. Taxable income funds may invest in all other debt securities. Bonds in these funds are generally issued by the United States federal government or its agencies (or a specific country's government, in the case of foreign bond funds), and can also include bonds issued by higher-rated corporations. Companies such as Standard & Poor's and Moody's assign ratings of quality to bonds issued around the world.

3. High-yield funds buy lower-rated corporate or municipal bonds. These bonds have a lower credit rating than do the higher rated "investment grade" bonds and may have a higher risk of default but will usually offer higher yields to compensate for the higher risk.

4. Money market funds invest in highly liquid short-term money market instruments, such as US Treasury bills.

These funds may be most appropriate for short-term goals, such as a down payment on a home, since they are among the least risky investments you can choose. However, you should note that an investment in a money market fund is generally not insured or guaranteed by the Federal Deposit Insurance Corp. (FDIC) or any other government agency. Although the fund seeks to preserve the value of your investment at $1.00 per share, it is possible to lose money by investing in the fund.

Think globally. Also keep in mind that global and international funds can help you diversify your portfolio among a wide array of foreign stocks and bonds. However, international investments may involve greater risks that do not apply to domestic investments, including currency risk and political uncertainty.

You should note that some tax-exempt fund holdings could be subject to the federal *alternative minimum tax*. Capital gains, if any, are taxable for federal and, in most cases, state purposes.

Understanding mutual fund categories is only the first step toward mutual fund investing. The next step is to match your personal goals, your time frame, and your risk tolerance to appropriate fund categories and build an asset allocation that is right for you. Getting the asset allocation right for your individual situation can be a difficult challenge for many investors, so you may want to seek guidance from a qualified financial professional.

FROM OUR FILES...

Do You Have the Right Stuff?

Many times, people invest money because someone sold them on an idea, not because it was the right thing to do. The investment may have sounded good that day. Maybe the investment salesperson was particularly persuasive that day. Maybe they were just not listening closely enough. Whatever the reasons, it is not uncommon to find people owning all sorts of investments that have no business in their portfolios because the investments are ill suited to do what needs to be done. In my professional practice, we see it all the time.

Let's go through a hypothetical story of Sue, an older investor. Sue's family was very concerned because she didn't have enough income to live on and yet she had significant assets. They approached a financial advisor for help. After researching her investments, the problem was easy to spot. Nothing in her portfolio was designed to do what she needed done. She owned nearly $1 million of LPs (limited partnership interests) that were illiquid, designed for growth over a long time frame, and produced almost no income. The illiquid nature of these LP interests meant that she was locked in to holding them for a very long period of time. If she tried to sell the LP interests, there was no active market for them, and any buyers would try to buy the LP interests for pennies on the dollar, taking advantage of the illiquid nature of the investment.

While it was possible that the investments could grow in value over time and eventually be worth much more than their original purchase price, the wait for that future value might render Sue in pretty dire straits financially while waiting for these investments to mature.

The same $1 million could have been invested in more-liquid investment vehicles that could have produced a comfortable income for Sue. The liquidity could have given her flexibility to adapt to changing circumstances. When the financial advisor pressed Sue for why she owned the investments she did, she told her advisor that the salesmen just made it sound so good.

Are there investments in your portfolio that are not designed to do what you need done? How much of your portfolio contains things that sounded good that day but have not performed up to expectations over time? It may be worth a second look at what you have. It may be time to get an independent review of your investments to make sure you are on the right track to accomplish your individual goals.

FINANCE 102:
Common Scenario Planning

III. PLANNING FOR TAXES

The Plan We All Need

This section of the book is a bit digressive, since virtually everything in this book has to do with taxes in one way or the other. In fact, you will see that really this chapter could be the *entire* book instead of the shortest chapter in it.

But as we all know from personal experiences, the one person who can disturb our financial peace of mind more than anyone else is the tax man. So in this brief chapter, we will cover a few of the key concepts that are important to know when discussing your taxes. We will also find ways that will make sure the advice you get may be made more useful with a little bit of detailed information.

Let's start by looking at *plans that allow us to control the impact taxes may have*. Some of these may be familiar to many readers, but let's look at them carefully and out of the context of the other chapters (notably the last chapter which deals with retirement) where these concepts could also easily appear.

CHAPTER 25

WHAT SHOULD I DO WITH THE MONEY IN MY 401(K), 403(B), OR OTHER PARTICIPANT-DIRECTED ACCOUNT? [1]

There are many tools to help you prepare for retirement, but few are as widely used as these plans. If you are eligible for a distribution from your employer's participant-directed retirement plan (401(k), 403(b), etc.), it is important that you understand your options and the advantages and disadvantages of each. This summary can help you identify some of the most important considerations.[2]

FOUR OPTIONS TO CONSIDER

There are four possible options for participants in these plans. The first three options allow you to continue to hold your retirement monies in a tax-deferred manner. The fourth option will subject your money to current taxes (and potentially to a 10 percent tax penalty).

---

1 These considerations were prepared for pre-tax 401(k) and 403(b) accounts. Some—but not all—of these considerations may also apply to other types of plans and/or accounts (e.g., Roth after-tax accounts). You should consult a tax advisor if you participate in a different type of plan or hold a different type of account.

2 IMPORTANT NOTE: These descriptions are for general educational purposes and should not be construed as advice or recommendations. This is not legal or tax advice, and plan participants should consult with their tax and legal advisors on these issues. This summary was prepared in June 2014 and does not reflect developments after that date.

Here is what you can do (and what your decision will mean):

1. You can keep your money in your plan.
2. You can roll over your money into an individual retirement account or annuity ("rollover IRA").
3. You can transfer your money to a new employer's retirement plan.
4. You can withdraw the money from your account.

Let's go over these one by one and look at some of the most important considerations for choosing among these:

OPTION 1: KEEP YOUR MONEY IN THE PLAN.

There may be some exceptions, but as a rule, you may leave your money in your plan and retain the pre-tax status (until it is ultimately distributed). However, some plans have mandatory distributions for accounts worth less than $5,000, so check with your plan administrator.

Advantages of Option 1:

- **Careful monitoring.** The federal law governing the plan—ERISA—requires that the plan fiduciaries prudently monitor the cost and quality of the investments options in the plan.
- **Other choices**. Your plan may offer investment choices and other services that are less expensive than those available to you outside of the plan.

- **Safety**. Employer-sponsored plans may offer better creditor protection than rollover IRAs (but both are protected in bankruptcy).
- **Flexibility.** If you have a participant loan, you may be able to continue to make payments on the loan rather than having to take a taxable distribution of the loan amount. However, some plans require payment of the loan when you leave your job, so check with your plan administrator.
- **Easy exits**. If you are at least fifty-five years old when you leave your job (or you are disabled), you may be eligible to take penalty-free withdrawals from the plan, but the withdrawals will be subject to ordinary income taxation.

Disadvantages of Option 1:

- **Less control**. You do not have control over the plan investments or services available to you. Your former employer, as the plan fiduciary, will make those decisions.
- **Limited choices.** The plan may offer a limited number of investment choices (unless it permits you to use a brokerage account).
- **Expenses**. The plan may assess fees to your account for administrative or other reasons.
- **On your own**. You may not have access through the plan to personalized investment advice or advice that takes into account your other assets or particular needs.

OPTION 2: ROLLOVER YOUR MONEY INTO AN IRA.

Another option for preserving the tax-deferred status of your retirement money is to transfer your 401(k) or 403(b) account to a rollover IRA. It is important to find out about the range of investments and services available through a particular IRA and the fees for that IRA before choosing your rollover IRA.

Advantages of Option 2:

- **Choice.** This is your account, and you have discretion over your money, including deciding which financial institution, investments, and services to use—and whether to make changes in the future.
- **Available advice.** An advisor for a rollover IRA may be able to give you personalized advice about investing and retirement planning.
- **Consolidation.** A rollover IRA may allow you to consolidate your other tax-deferred retirement accounts in one place. This may be helpful for your financial and retirement planning. It may also prove helpful in managing the required minimum distributions you will have to start taking when you reach seventy and a half.
- **Professional help.** A rollover IRA may also enable you to place all your investments with one advisor, who may be able to better coordinate your overall financial and investment planning.
- **Added flexibility.** IRAs are often more flexible than employer plans on withdrawals and distributions—e.g., setting up regular periodic payments or an unscheduled withdrawal.

- **Portable**. IRAs are easily transferable between financial institutions—so if you decide you don't like the one you are with, changing to another provider is usually easy.
- **Security**. If you select an individual retirement annuity, you can obtain a guarantee of lifetime income. However, there are many other factors and risks to consider, such as fees, surrender charges. Also, the guarantees are contingent on the claims-paying ability of the issuing insurance company.

Disadvantages of Option 2:

- **Many variables**. There is no plan fiduciary who prudently monitors the investments and their cost and quality in your rollover IRA. Also, there will usually be more choices through an IRA, and you will need to select your own investments. However, if you have an advisor for your IRA, he or she can help you with the investment decisions.
- **Added costs**. You may pay more in a rollover IRA for investments, services, and advice than you pay through your retirement plan (or a successor plan). Compare those costs to your plan's fees for services, investments, and administration.
- **Inflexible funding**. You cannot borrow from an IRA—you can only access the money in an IRA by taking a taxable distribution (which may also subject you to tax penalties if you are younger than fifty-nine and a half).
- **Vulnerable**. Generally, rollover IRAs are protected in bankruptcy but may not otherwise offer the same level of creditor protection as employer-sponsored retirement plans.

OPTION 3: TRANSFER YOUR MONEY
TO A NEW EMPLOYER'S PLAN.

The third way to preserve the tax-deferred benefit of your 401(k) or 403(b) account is to transfer the money in your account to a new employer's plan. While most employer plans allow new employees to roll their accounts in, not all do, so it is important that you ask. (Obviously, this option is not available if you are retiring and will not be working for a new employer.)

Advantages of Option 3:

- **Simplicity**. You will be able to make contributions to your participant-directed account at your new employer when you become eligible to participate in that plan and, as a result, you can have all of your retirement plan monies in one place.
- **Lower costs**. The new plan could potentially offer lower-cost investment options and services.
- **Loan provisions.** Many plans have loan provisions. If you transfer your retirement funds to a new employer's plan that permits loans, you may be able to borrow from the money in the new plan.
- **Direct rollover**. If you have an existing loan, you may be able to roll it over to your new employer's plan through a "direct" rollover. Check with the plan administrator at both your former employer and your new employer.
- **Added protections**. In some states, employer-sponsored retirement plans offer better creditor protection than IRAs. (However, both rollover IRAs and participant-directed plans are protected under federal bankruptcy

laws.) Keeping your retirement money in another employer-sponsored plan helps you maintain the creditor protection.

- **Transparent**. You should ask about the administrative and other fees assessed to participants' accounts in the new employer's plan and compare them to your alternatives.

- **No mandatory distributions**. So long as you are working at the employer, you will not be required to take minimum distributions when you reach seventy and a half (unless you are a 5 percent or more owner of the business).

Disadvantages of Option 3:

- **Limits on rollovers**. The new plan may not allow rollovers or, if it does, there may be a waiting period.

- **Inflexible**. The new plan might offer fewer or more expensive options than your former plan. Make sure that the option you choose has the right investments (at the right cost) for your needs.

- **No help**. The new plan may not offer personalized advice on investments or retirement planning.

- **Little control**. You will not have control over the expenses, services, or investments in the new plan.

OPTION 4: WITHDRAW YOUR MONEY FROM YOUR ACCOUNT.

It is your money and you get to choose what is right for you. One decision you could make is to simply take a taxable distribution.

Advantages of Option 4:

- **Freedom**. You can use the money as you wish—for example, to pay off existing debt, bills, or other expenses.
- **Tax-free possibilities**. If you have made after-tax contributions (other than Roth contributions), you will be able to take these amounts tax-free (though you will be required to pay tax on the earnings on those amounts). (There are special rules for Roth contributions and, depending on the circumstances, they may or may not be taxable if withdrawn from a plan.)
- **Shareholder advantages**. If you have employer stock that is substantially appreciated, there may be significant tax advantages in taking a distribution of those shares. Check with your tax advisor.

Disadvantages of Option 4:

- **Taxes**. You will owe federal (and possibly state) income taxes on the money you withdraw. The government requires 20 percent withholding for federal income taxes, so the amount you receive will automatically be reduced. Also, the withdrawn money could put you in a higher tax bracket, and you may owe even more taxes.

- **More taxes**. If you are under the age of fifty-nine and a half, you would also owe 10 percent early distribution tax penalty, in addition to the income taxes.
- **Your retirement account is empty**. Once you spend the withdrawal, you will need to begin saving for retirement again, but with fewer years left to save—and without the spent savings, it may delay your retirement date or result in a lower standard of living in retirement.

CHAPTER 26

DO I NEED TO TAKE MONEY OUT OF MY RETIREMENT ACCOUNTS AFTER SEVENTY?

When you reach age seventy-two, the Internal Revenue Service has very specific rules that require you to begin taking at least a specified amount of money each year from your retirement accounts. This specified required amount is called a *required minimum distribution,* or RMD.

In the year you turn seventy-two, you are expected to take a minimum distribution either that year or the following year. For every year thereafter, you must take the required minimum distribution by December 31 of each tax year.

IRS Publication 590. The actual amount of this required minimum distribution is calculated using an IRS table available in IRS publication number 590. You can download a copy of publication number 590 for free from the IRS website at www.irs.gov. The IRS's calculation is based on a factor from an IRS table and is applied to your total retirement account balance as of December 31 of the prior year.

It is extremely important to get this calculation right, as there is a 50 percent penalty tax for not withdrawing the proper amount by the IRS deadline. It is one thing to have to withdraw the money and pay income taxes, but to pay a 50 percent penalty tax on top of that is just awful! So, you want to get this one right!

Consolidating your accounts. If you have multiple accounts at several financial institutions, you may want to strongly consider consolidating these various accounts into one to avoid the risk of not getting the calculation right. You see, from the IRS's point of view, it is as if you only had one retirement account. The required minimum distribution amount is ultimately calculated on the aggregate balance of all of your retirement accounts.

If you only have one account, the calculation is fairly easy, and there is less chance for error. But if you have many accounts spread over many financial institutions, getting the RMD calculation correct may be more difficult. The bottom line is that required minimum distributions from retirement accounts are a fact of life under current tax law. You have to take your money, like it or not.

Just be sure to seek help to get the calculation done right and get the proper amount withdrawn from your account before the IRS deadline.

As I mentioned earlier, many things in this book touch on tax considerations—especially as they concern retirement. But some rules deserve a special spotlight. The following chapter focuses on one of those rules.

CHAPTER 27

DO I HAVE TO PAY TAXES ON MONEY I WITHDRAW FROM AN IRA ACCOUNT?

Do you know the answers to the following questions?

1. Can you withdraw money from an IRA account and not have to pay taxes on it?
2. If you do withdraw money from an IRA account, can you put the money back in the account without paying taxes on it?

These are actually very tricky questions. Here is the main thing you need to know: If you withdraw money from your IRA and then redeposit that money within sixty days from the date of the withdrawal, you can avoid paying income taxes on the withdrawal. This is called the sixty day rule.

This is an important rule because when you withdraw money from an IRA account, generally it is a taxable event. You will pay federal income taxes. Depending on the state you consider your home for tax purposes, you may also have to pay state income taxes. If you are under age fifty-nine and a half, generally you will also pay a 10 percent penalty tax for early withdrawal of retirement funds.

So depending on where you live, tapping your IRA account could mean giving up nearly 50 percent of your withdrawal to income taxes. That is expensive money!

But there are some ways around it. The sixty day rule is one.

A short-term loan. If you are in need of a very short-term loan and you are sure you can pay the loan back quickly, this might be an option to just borrow the money from yourself and then pay it back before the 60-day time clock runs out. Just do not imagine there is any grace period.

The IRS tends to be inflexible on this sixty day rule. At sixty-one days, you will pay the full tax and penalties, if applicable. Another application of the sixty day rule comes into play when you are transferring money from one IRA account to another IRA account.

Be sure to get the money deposited in the new account within the 60-day time limit. Better yet, have the old account balance directly transferred to the new account and deposited for you.

If you do not physically receive the check, then the sixty day rule does not apply. If you are leaving an employer and getting a distribution from the company's retirement plan, have them send your distribution directly to your IRA rollover account or to your new employer's retirement plan. That way, you completely avoid paying any income taxes on the transfer and the sixty day rule does not apply.

Your financial professional can help explain taxes as they relate to your financial plan, so do not hesitate to ask for help when you need it. The tax code was four hundred pages long when it was unveiled in 1913. By 2013, it had swollen to 73,954 pages, according to an illustrated chart titled "Federal Tax Laws Keep Piling Up" in the *CCH Standard Federal Tax Reporter*. Those are a lot of rules that citizens must obey, so be sure to also seek professional guidance from a qualified tax advisor. This may not only be prudent, it may be essential.

This short chapter highlights some of the tax implications in planning for peace of mind. If you only take away one important fact about taxes, it is this: They cannot be avoided. But they can be managed—as part of a comprehensive plan.

FINANCE 102:
Common Scenario Planning

IV. PLANNING FOR THE NEXT GENERATION

Now let's turn our attention to a very important topic that affects you and everyone you care about. I am talking about estate-planning and other preparation for your future. It has been said that there are only two sure things in life: death and taxes. When we are taken from this earth, we leave behind many things, including assets accumulated over our lifetimes. Without a plan to distribute those assets to take care of our families and benefit those we love, things can get very messy for those we leave behind and for some, the tax burden can be onerous. Everyone, regardless of how much wealth they have accumulated (or not), needs to have an estate plan. This estate plan should create a comprehensive framework for dealing with death, disability, cognitive impairment, and other things that life can send our way. Let's take a look at some of the things you should consider.

CHAPTER 28

DO I NEED AN ESTATE PLAN?

We all know that estate-planning matters. Most people seem to understand, at least intellectually, that they need an estate plan. They have some vague concept that they need a will. They often have an even vaguer notion of when they might get around to getting a will prepared. No doubt because the subject doesn't really give rise to pleasant thoughts, a shocking percentage of Americans do not have a will or any other estate-planning documents in place.

From my own observation and professional experience, I can tell you that for an adult in the United States to die without any estate plan is a real tragedy. I firmly believe that one of the most loving things you can do for your family is to get your estate-planning affairs in order.

There are many reasons for this, but for starters, losing a loved one is hard enough. There is often a long, painful grieving process. Lack of a well-thought-out estate plan can quickly complicate the lives of those left behind. Loved ones are forced to deal with a mess created because there was no plan. To make matters worse, there is Murphy's Law: "Anything that can go wrong, will go wrong."

The spouse who normally deals with the family's financial, legal, and tax issues is all too often the one who dies first. You see, in most families, one or the other spouse tends to look after the financial affairs of the family. This is not about male and female roles; this is just the reality of how many families operate.

If the spouse who usually handles things dies first, the surviving spouse is left with what may seem to be a pool of quicksand in which they are slowly sinking. Most of this additional confusion, complication, and hassle is avoidable with a properly prepared and executed estate plan.

If you care what happens to your family after you are gone, then get started on your estate plan today. Begin to make notes on whom you would want to act in your behalf if you are not there to take care of things. Who would you want to receive some or all of your savings and investments after you are gone? Who should get any real estate you own? What organizations do you support that you might want to leave a bequest to further their mission?

Deciding who gets what and when they get it after your death is just one small part of the estate-planning process. Death is only one possibility on a list of other life possibilities, such as disability, incapacity, divorce, remarriage, care of minor children or grandchildren, and so much more. Each of these can be addressed with a properly crafted overall estate plan.

If you want to give your family one of the ultimate gifts in life that you have the power to bestow, getting your estate plan in place is that gift. An estate plan is a gift of love in a most powerful way.

Let's review the basic elements of a well-designed estate plan. First, let's look at wills and trusts and how they are used.

CHAPTER 29

SHOULD I DRAFT A WILL, A TRUST, OR BOTH?

When preparing an estate plan, one of the strategic decisions you will have to make, with the help of your estate-planning attorney, is whether to have a will, a trust, or both.

Here are the differences and why you might choose one over the other.

A will is a document that spells out your wishes about the disposition of your estate after your death. Everything you own, including real estate, personal property, bank accounts, investment accounts, retirement accounts, etc., is your estate. Everything you own must be given away or disposed of in some way after your death. Who gets what and how they get it can be spelled out to suit your wishes.

A living trust can serve as a will substitute. A living trust can do everything a will can do plus it can help you avoid the probate process, keep your affairs private, and make transitions easier on those who are left behind. So what is the difference in the two?

One important difference is in the handling of the estate after your death.

A will typically needs to be handled by an estate attorney and will often involve the probate court to disperse your estate according to the terms of your will. This can be an expensive, time-consuming process and is a very public process. The records of the probate court are available for public viewing.

Your nosy neighbor can go to the courthouse and look at a list of your assets as disclosed to the court. Assets have to be re-registered in the name of the new owner, and deeds have to be prepared to change ownership on real estate. The paperwork involved can be overwhelming. Then there are the costs. Attorney's fees and court fees can add up fast.

Contrast this scenario with a living trust.

With a living trust, most or all of your assets are titled in the name of the trust. You control the trust and have the full use and benefit of the trust's assets during your lifetime. At your death, your successor trustee takes control of the assets in the trust and distributes them as you have directed. There is very little, if any, probate process. There are very little, if any, attorney costs. It is just a smooth transition without too much fuss.

So, a will is a simple, fairly low-cost document to prepare and fairly expensive on the back end to administer. A trust is a little more costly on the front end, with little cost or fuss to administer on the back end. Plus, a trust can be entirely private, so a nosy neighbor has no opportunity to look into your affairs.

Will or trust? You and your estate-planning attorney can decide what is best for your individual situation. However, here is an important caveat. Estate-planning is a very specialized area of law. It is important to work with an experienced estate-planning attorney—a specialist—to advise you and prepare documents for you.

CHAPTER 30

WHAT ARE THE BENEFITS OF USING TRUSTS TO DISTRIBUTE MY ESTATE?

In your estate plan, you may have a will or a living trust that details your wishes on how your estate will be distributed to your heirs after your death.

All too frequently, these documents are prepared with a child or other non-spouse beneficiary receiving a direct gift from the estate. The reason I mentioned children and non-spouse beneficiaries specifically is that the rules for gifts to a spouse are different than a gift to any other person. I will discuss gift rules for your spouse later.

1. Asset protection.

In the case of a child or other non-spouse beneficiary, a direct gift is simply giving the money or other asset directly to the child or other non-spouse beneficiary. It would be the same as just handing your child a pile of cash and then hoping they will use it wisely. They could spend the cash, they could give away the cash, they could give up some of the money in a divorce, or a creditor could take away the cash. In other words, the direct gift is fully exposed to a number of risks. So, the first reason you should use trusts to make estate gifts to children is financial protection.

Here is how this trust design works to protect your gift. *A gift in trust is not a gift directly to the child.* The trust is a separate legal entity and is not part of the child's personal property. You can name the child as the beneficiary of the trust. You can even name the child as the trustee of the trust. In this context, a trustee of the trust is the person who controls the trust. In other words, your child could have the full use and benefit of the gift without actually owning the gift. This lack of direct ownership could be very important from a financial protection point of view.

For example, if your child was involved in an accident and there were damages to be paid, the child's personal assets might be at risk, but the trust would not be accessible to creditors. Or if your child were involved in a divorce proceeding, the child's personal assets might be subject to division by the court, but the trust assets would be protected.

2. Ease of administration.

The second reason you should use trusts to make estate gifts to your children is ease of administration.

Specifically, you can name a successor trustee for the trust. If your child were to die or become disabled, the successor trustee could step in and take over administration of the trust without too much fuss or hassle. No assets would have to be retitled, no accounts would have to be transferred, and there would be no probate court involved to oversee administration of the trust. Transition is quick, easy, and smooth.

3. Lighter tax burden.

The third reason why you should use trusts to make estate gifts to your children is potential estate tax savings. Since the trust is not the personal property of your child, it is not part of his or her estate and therefore not subject to estate taxes under current law.

Of course, every estate-planning situation is unique, so be sure to consult your estate-planning attorney for details on the use of trusts to make gifts to children or other non-spouse beneficiaries and to make sure this is the right approach for you.

Leaving a gift to a spouse.

Now, let's discuss briefly the rules for gifts to a spouse. Under current law, you can give an unlimited amount of money and property to your spouse. This is referred to as the unlimited marital deduction. If a gift is made at your death, there are special considerations that could affect how that gift or the appreciation of that gift over time might be taxed. Aside from tax considerations, some aspects of the asset protection and ease of administration using trusts discussed above would still apply. However, gifts to spouses need to be carefully considered and discussed thoroughly with your estate-planning attorney to explore what would work best in your situation.

CHAPTER 31

DO I NEED A LIVING WILL?

What would happen if you needed emergency medical care and you could not make decisions about your care or communicate your wishes? Who would speak for you? Who would make critical health care decisions that would be in your best interest?

An unpleasant truth is that there are situations where decisions must be made, and these decisions could have a "life or death" impact on us. For example, advancements in medical technology now enable doctors to keep us alive in ways that were unimaginable just a few years ago.

Maybe you do not want to think about it, but consider for a moment what if you were completely incapacitated, perhaps on life support, with no hope for recovery? Would you want your family and your doctor to keep you alive, sometimes at an incredible financial cost that can drain the family's finances, even if you have no conscious awareness, no quality of life, and no chance for a recovery?

Many people look at that situation and answer no and say they would want *someone* to "just pull the plug" under those circumstances. But exactly who would make that decision?

In a less-dire circumstance, what would happen if you were unconscious after an accident and were unable to authorize desperately needed surgery? Who would you want to make this important health care decision for you? You owe it to yourself and your loved ones to make this important decision *now*—before the need occurs.

BY ANY OTHER NAME...

Your estate-planning attorney can work with you to create a document authorizing someone you trust to make health care decisions in case you cannot do that for yourself. A living will, sometimes called a statement to physician, heath care proxy, or health care power of attorney, is an important part of your estate-planning.

This is a document you create and then hope will never be needed, because if you need it, you are ill enough that you need someone else to make health care decisions for you.

If you don't already have a living will or other document that authorizes someone you trust to make health care decisions in case you cannot do that for yourself, make it a priority. Get it done and have the peace of mind that you and your loved ones are protected and that your wishes will be honored.

CHAPTER 32

WHO SHOULD MANAGE MY AFFAIRS IF I BECOME INCAPACITATED?

It is said that there are only two sure things in life: death and taxes.

For financial planning purposes, however, there is another certainty—in fact, there is a pretty long list of possible occurrences that you should consider before they happen. Take disability, for example. If you are ever incapacitated for some period of time, you may need some legal help to manage your affairs. If you cannot sign checks or tax returns, you may need some help to look after the business of your life.

A simple, low-cost way of handling such a possibility is have your estate-planning attorney create a durable power of attorney as part of your estate-planning documents. This legal document *gives the person you name the power to act on your behalf, in the event that you are incapacitated and unable to handle your own affairs.* In a typical husband and wife situation, each spouse will name the other partner.

This is another one of those documents that you prepare and hope you will never need. At the appropriate time, however, the absence of this document can result in a messy and expensive situation for those who love you and want to take care of you. If you were incapacitated and had not executed a power of attorney, your spouse might have to take legal action to be appointed your guardian and be granted the power to look after your personal affairs.

This would, in many circumstances, include hiring an attorney and petitioning the court to declare you incompetent to handle your own affairs. This process, which can be time consuming and emotionally draining, is totally avoidable.

If you do not already have an up-to-date durable power of attorney on file, make it a priority to get one prepared right away. You will be glad you did. And those who love you will thank you if the document is ever needed.

CHAPTER 33

HOW CAN I MAKE SURE DEATH BENEFIT PROCEEDS AREN'T TAXED AS PART OF MY ESTATE?

Many people own life insurance. Perhaps you do too. But have you ever thought about the importance of *who owns the policy and who is named as beneficiary*? These important questions should be carefully considered. We discussed beneficiaries in an earlier chapter, but let us take a look at a typical situation, one we see all the time in working with clients.

Let us say our client owns a life insurance policy on himself or herself, and the spouse is named as the beneficiary. The client's intent was to provide additional cash to supplement other savings and investments to ensure that the spouse would be well taken care of in the event of the client's untimely death. This is all too common. This might even be your situation. But here is the problem.

You might be throwing money away.

If you own a life insurance policy, the entire death benefit proceeds going to your beneficiary may be included in your estate for calculating estate taxes. This means that as much as half of the life insurance you are paying for may be effectively wasted because it is going to be taxed as a part of your estate. That could mean that half of the money you intended to be available to protect your spouse might just evaporate into thin air as it goes to pay unnecessary taxes.

Doesn't sound promising, does it? Well, here is an alternative. There is a special type of trust designed to more efficiently own life insurance from an estate tax perspective and eliminate some or all of these problems.

AN ALTERNATIVE: THE IRREVOCABLE LIFE INSURANCE TRUST.

This special trust is called an irrevocable life insurance trust or ILIT. If you create such a trust, the ILIT can be the owner of a life insurance policy on you. The key point here is that the ILIT is the owner of the policy, *not you personally*. The trust is also the beneficiary of the policy.

Your spouse can be named as trustee of the trust, giving your spouse full control of the trust and the death benefit payments from the life insurance policy. Because the trust is the owner of the policy, the death benefit is *not* included in your estate tax calculation, and there is no estate tax to be paid on this particular money you have set aside for the benefit of your spouse.

At your death, the death benefit is paid to the ILIT, and your spouse takes control of the funds as trustee of the ILIT. Your spouse is free to use these funds as needed to help take care of themselves, your family, and the things that are important to you.

Further, *the death benefit money can be protected from creditors by the terms of the trust*. Your spouse has full control of and full use of the life insurance death benefit. This control and protection from creditors can be passed down to the next generation simply by adding the appropriate language to the trust document.

If you are going to own life insurance, talk with your estate-planning attorney about the benefits and limitations of using an irrevocable life insurance trust to be the owner and beneficiary of that life insurance.

CHAPTER 34

HOW CAN I PREVENT DISCORD AMONG FAMILY MEMBERS AS MY ESTATE IS DISTRIBUTED?

When preparing a will or living trust as a part of an estate plan, many people focus just on the terms of how their estate will be distributed after their death.

However, if there are multiple heirs, there may be the possibility for conflict if one beneficiary feels they did not get what they thought they deserved. One fairly easy and low-cost way to eliminate, or at least substantially reduce, any chance for dissension and discord as your estate is administered, is to have your attorney add a "no contest clause" to your will or trust document.

The anti-bickering device.

What this "no contest" clause typically says is that you have clearly stated your intentions for the disposition of your estate, and that any beneficiary is free to challenge the estate plan, but their inheritance will be reduced to $1 if they contest the estate plan.

In my experience, any disgruntled heir will suddenly get very cooperative and compliant when they learn that they are about to see their inheritance reduced to just one dollar.

Adding a "no contest" clause is a simple, low-cost way of insuring that your wishes are carried out and that your heirs have no room for bickering about your choices.

CHAPTER 35

WHAT DOCUMENTS SHOULD I PREPARE IN ADDITION TO MY ESTATE PLAN?

If you are one of the smart, savvy people that have already created an estate plan to protect your family and your assets, congratulations! You are to be commended for your efforts, and I assure you that your family will thank you over and over for having taken the time to document clear instructions for the disposition of your assets.

However, there are a couple of things you can do that will really enhance the work you have already done.

WHAT YOU NEED NOW

A short list of things you must have in place now:

1. Make a list of things that your spouse or other heirs will need to know—a "List of Important Information."
2. Write a "Letter of Instruction" about what you want done in the event of your death.

Neither of these will cost you anything except a little bit of your time. One thing you can do is create a "List of Important Information," and make it accessible to your spouse or another trusted family member or friend.

List of important information.

Your "list of important information" is just what it sounds like. It is a list of the information that would definitely be valuable to your surviving loved ones. It contains whom to call in the event of an emergency or death. Each name should be listed with full contact information and a brief description of the role this person or organization plays in your life. For example, you might list your banker, your life insurance agent, your financial advisor, your minister, and so on.

You might list your bank accounts, brokerage accounts, retirement accounts, insurance policies, and so on, along with a contact name for each account, account numbers, and online usernames and passwords, if applicable.

In this digital age, you should list passwords to online accounts, websites, and social media sites—in fact, any site for which you have a username and password for access should be on this list. Again, listing all this information doesn't cost you anything but a small portion of your time. But as you can imagine, the time savings for your surviving family members will be enormous.

You can do it as a handwritten list that you update as needed, or better yet, create a secure file on your personal computer and update the list regularly. Let your family know the list exists, and keep a printed copy in your bank lock box or other secure location, along with copies of your will, trusts, and other estate -planning documents.

This list of important information will be of incalculable value to those you leave behind. This list will help your family know that every aspect of your affairs has been taken care of in the way you intended, and there is nothing left for them to worry about or be surprised by.

The letter of instruction.

Another very valuable document you can create and maintain on your own is what I call a "letter of instruction" to your spouse or to your family. This is a letter that you write to your spouse or other heirs that gives them insight about your intentions, your desires, and your dreams for them. If you own a business, this letter can help them understand your intentions about the continuation of that business and treatment of your business partners. In this letter, you can spell out your wishes on the disposition or use of real property you own.

Maybe you've already discussed much of this with them. But your letter will make these wishes fresh and help them to understand your intention for the disposition of your personal property. If you have a cherished gun collection, stamp collection, or other such collection, name the child or grandchild you want to have which item. Do not leave things you care about up for grabs. If there are certain tools, pieces of furniture, art, jewelry, collectibles, and the like that you want to go to certain people, you can easily make your intentions known in this letter of instruction. Since this is a confidential document you create and maintain on your own, you can change it any time you like.

If you take the time to read your will or trust documents created for your estate plan, most attorneys mention such a list or letter by reference. In this way, you do not have to keep updating your estate plan every time you acquire something new or dispose of something—you can just update your own letter of instruction and your letter of instruction. If your will or trust does not have such a reference to refer to your letter of instruction and letter of instruction, ask your attorney to add appropriate language to your document.

Consider these documents gifts.

Creating a list of important information and a letter of instruction does not cost anything but your time and attention to do it initially, or to maintain and update them over time. I know from personal experience that creating and maintaining these documents is not difficult or time consuming. But the benefits to those you care about most are enormous.

Speaking from conviction...

I have been doing this for years, and it has brought great comfort to my wife to know that she will always have the information she needs when the time comes. I also know from my professional experience that those families who had access to this kind of information said it made all the difference in making the transition easier.

It is hard enough to lose a loved one, and creating these documents is a loving, caring act you can do to better take care of your family. You will be glad you did, and your family will be truly grateful to you for having done it.

CHAPTER 36

HOW OFTEN SHOULD I REVIEW MY ESTATE PLAN?

Once you get your estate plan in place, do not just tuck it away in the bank lock box and never look at it again. We recommend to our clients to review their estate plan at least **every three years.**

Leave nothing to chance.

Take the time to actually read the documents again. Do they say what you intended? Do you still feel the same way you did as when they were originally prepared? After you are satisfied that the documents reflect your current thinking or you have made notes on what changes are needed, have your estate-planning attorney review the documents to make sure they still meet the requirements of current tax laws and other legal considerations.

If you get into the habit of reviewing your estate plan every three years, you will never be too far off base. You will go a long way to ensuring a smooth transition for those who are left behind after your time on this earth is done.

FROM OUR FILES...

Do You Know What You Have in Your Estate?

Finding out can be rewarding.

Allen and Martha met with their financial advisor to help them get their affairs in order. They began working together, gathering detailed information on their assets, income, insurance, estate-planning, and much more. It became clear to the financial advisor very quickly that Allen and Martha were both quite disorganized in their record keeping and handling of their financial affairs in general.

Allen was a busy, successful professional who was constantly bombarded with phone calls from investment brokers and insurance salesmen offering him the "hot deal of the day" in one form or another. He often bought "what sounded good that day" and this led to an investment portfolio that was a messy mix of discon-nected pieces that together did not seem to make sense relative to what they were sharing about their goals and dreams for the future.

Every time their financial advisor thought he had assembled a complete picture of all of their assets, Allen would remember one more thing that he had failed to tell the advisor about. Finally, the advisor suggested that he visit their home and help them sort it all out. All of their financial records were kept in Allen's study, so they went there to see what else they could find. After several hours of sorting through file drawers full of papers, they reached a place that they both agreed they had been through every file and paper as thoroughly as one could hope to do.

Not only did completing the information-gathering process allow the advisor to begin analysis of their situation, but they also found over a quarter of a million dollars' worth of assets Allen had simply forgotten about. Even for a successful man like Allen, losing track of over $250,000 could have an important impact on one's financial affairs. Allen and Martha were ecstatic over finding the hidden assets and feeling like they were getting in control of their financial future.

FINANCE 102:
Common Scenario Planning

V. PLANNING FOR RETIREMENT

Now that we have looked at four of the five key plans you need for financial peace of mind, let's turn our attention to the fifth: retirement planning. It may be the last plan in this book, but I hope it is not last in your thinking.

How much do you need? This is often the first question many people have about retirement, and for good reason. The answer will determine the level of income you will need to support the retirement lifestyle of your dreams.

There are rules of thumb for this. For example, many financial experts suggest that most people will be very comfortable maintaining their pre-retirement lifestyle on about 70 to 80 percent of their pre-retirement income. In determining your ideal level of retirement income, do not forget to factor how increasing inflation can gradually erode the purchasing power of your dollars.

CHAPTER 37

HOW DOES INFLATION IMPACT MY RETIREMENT INCOME?

The impact of inflation on your retirement income can be enormous. Let's suppose you decide you need $50,000 per year in gross income to live comfortably in retirement. Let's further suppose that we project an inflation rate of 3 percent per year. For reference, the average rate of inflation in the United States over the past eighty years or so is around 3 percent.

- Just ten years into your retirement, you will need more than $67,000 to buy the same goods and services as you can buy today for $50,000.
- At twenty years into your retirement, you will need more than $90,000 to buy what $50,000 buys today.
- At thirty years into your retirement, you will need more than $121,000 to buy a $50,000 lifestyle in today's dollars.

So, when you are thinking about long-term retirement planning, do not forget to factor in the impact of inflation over time. If you are still several years away from retirement, you will still need to calculate the impact of inflation over time as you project how much you will need at retirement.

If your retirement is ten or twenty years away, it is very likely that you will need many more dollars of income than you do today. As long as there is inflation, keeping an eye on the purchasing power of your dollars will be critical to your long-term financial success.

CHAPTER 38

SHOULD I ASSIGN BENEFICIARY DESIGNATIONS FOR MY RETIREMENT ACCOUNTS?

We talked about beneficiary designations earlier in the book regarding insurance policies, but it's important to consider the subject again here in the context of retirement planning.

Many people don't think too much about the importance of beneficiary designations on retirement accounts. But they should. And so should you. You see, most forms of retirement accounts, such as IRA accounts, 401(k) accounts, and so on, need to have up-to-date beneficiary designations on file with the plan sponsor.

In the case of IRA accounts, the beneficiary designation should be on file with the financial institution handling the account. Your financial advisor might also keep this information in their files.

In the case of 401(k) and other employer-sponsored retirement plan accounts, the beneficiary designation should be on file with the employer and the custodian of the retirement plan.

WHO SHOULD BENEFIT?

A beneficiary designation is your legal instruction as to who should get the money in your account if you were to die prior to using the money yourself.

Many people will designate a spouse or a child as a beneficiary, and do so without even giving the matter a second thought. The problem with this is that there are legal, and often tax issues, to be considered when choosing beneficiaries for retirement accounts.

Make sure your beneficiary is legally able to benefit.

Even if the naming of a beneficiary was a well-informed choice at the time, it is important to keep the beneficiary designations up-to-date with changing circumstances. For example, we often find people have retirement accounts they have had for a very long time, and they haven't actually looked at the beneficiary information in many years. When we do a review of their investment and retirement accounts, we often discover things like an ex-spouse, or even a deceased person, still named as a beneficiary. Or we find a minor child named as a beneficiary.

As noted, when it comes to retirement accounts of any kind, typically the ideal primary beneficiary is your spouse and then your children as secondary beneficiaries. This is usually a good choice. The point here is that living persons make the best kind of beneficiaries for retirement accounts. If you have a trust created as a part of your estate-planning, the trust may be a beneficiary of last resort because of the difference in the way the tax laws treat living persons vs. trusts. A qualified charity could also be a beneficiary of a retirement account.

You should consult your estate-planning attorney or other appropriate advisor for guidance on naming beneficiaries.

You have control.

Now the good news is that the owner of the retirement plan account has the power to easily change a beneficiary and, usually, it is a fairly easy process. The account owner asks for a change of beneficiary form from the plan sponsor or custodian of the account. The form is completed and submitted to the plan sponsor or custodian, and the change is made. It is normally as simple as that.

Retirement accounts can be a valuable financial tool in your overall financial plan and can provide cash to meet a variety of needs. Why not take a few moments to check that your retirement accounts will end up in the hands of those you intended?

CHAPTER 39

HOW DO I TRANSFER A RETIREMENT ACCOUNT?

It happens all the time in this fast-paced, mobile society we live in. People change jobs and have a balance in an employer-sponsored retirement plan with the prior employer. They are leaving one job and moving to another. If that is happening or did happen to you, here are hints on how to handle the situation.

One important issue you should consider is what to do with the money in your 401(k) account. You could just leave your money in the current plan, but there are other options you should consider. Here are the facts you need to know:

Portability.

Are you moving from one job directly to another job? Does your new employer have a retirement plan that will accept rollovers from your previous employer's plan? If you answered "yes" to both questions, then moving your account balance to your new employer's plan may be your best option. If you missed the discussion of retirement plans in the section devoted to taxes (chapter 26), take a look now.

An IRA rollover account is a good idea if you have some time in between jobs or your new employer does not have a retirement plan. This type of account lets you park your retirement savings in a safe place where it is protected from taxes and will continue to grow and compound for you.

What Is an IRA Rollover Account?

An IRA rollover account is an Individual Retirement Account designed specifically to accept amounts paid out from employer-sponsored retirement plans. In most cases, you can elect to transfer the money in your IRA rollover account to you new employer's plan at a future date.

The next option is one you should generally *not* consider. Whatever you do, do not just cash in the retirement account and take the money. This can be a very expensive mistake that is easily avoided. Again, see chapters 25 through 27 for a more robust explanation, since the IRS has very specific rules about what you can and cannot do.

Moving Your Money

There are two ways to move money—with a transfer or with a rollover. These terms are sometimes used interchangeably, but there are some small but important differences of which you should be aware.

In a **direct transfer** of the account, Financial Institution A directly transfers the money to Financial Institution B. This may happen electronically or in the form of a check made payable to Financial Institution B (often referred to as an FBO check, because it is payable to the institution For the Benefit Of you). Either way, you do not have access to the money in the transfer process.

In a **rollover**, Financial Institution A gives you a check, payable to you, in the amount of your retirement account balance. You then deliver the check to Financial Institution B for deposit to your new account.

But be careful. *If you do not deposit the check in your new retirement account quickly enough, you may be subject to income taxes and other penalties.* Both transfer and rollover are acceptable procedures to the IRS. Neither will require you to pay income taxes on the transfer process, if executed properly.

However, it is almost always better to make sure the money moves directly between the financial institutions involved.

If you get your hands on the money in the form of a check made out to you, make a quick trip to get that money deposited in your new account to avoid taxes and penalties that may apply. Whether it is a rollover or a transfer, just make sure you get the money moved in the right way and avoid paying taxes and penalties. See the section on taxes for a discussion of the IRS's sixty day rule.

CHAPTER 40

HOW DO I GET THE MOST FROM MY RETIREMENT ACCOUNTS?

HERE ARE TEN WAYS YOU CAN GET MORE FROM YOUR RETIREMENT ACCOUNTS.

1. Capitalize on employer-sponsored retirement plans, such as 401(k) plans.

If you are employed and your employer offers a 401(k), 403(b), or other type of retirement savings plan, generally these are the retirement accounts that you should fund *first*, even before IRA or Roth IRA accounts.

Many of these plans offer "matching" funds from the employer to provide incentive for your participation. Participating in the plan and contributing enough to qualify for the match is vitally important. This is basically your employer offering you "free money" that you would not otherwise be able to access. All you have to do is participate in the plan and contribute at least enough to qualify for the match.

Rule of thumb: Generally, it is best to fully fund an employer-sponsored retirement plan before considering other retirement savings vehicles.

2. Take advantage of Roth 401(k) accounts in 401(k) retirement plans.

Some employers who offer 401(k) plans have added a Roth 401(k) provision. If you are younger than age fifty-five, you should consider using the Roth feature to save for retirement. This is because you can withdraw money from your Roth 401(k) account in retirement completely free from federal income taxes for the balance of your lifetime. You can also leave your Roth account to heirs, and withdrawals from the account will continue to be tax-free for your heirs.

Plus, some highly compensated workers can have a Roth 401(k) account even though their income is too high to qualify for a regular Roth IRA account. If you do not know what a Roth IRA is, see below.

3. Convert a regular 401(k) to a Roth 401(k) account.

As a result of tax legislation passed in 2013, you may be able to convert some or all of your regular 401(k) account to a Roth 401(k) account, if your employer's plan permits the conversion. This may work well if you have the available cash in other savings accounts to pay the income tax on the conversion. Again, consider your age at the time of conversion. The younger you are, the more it may make sense to do the conversion.

Of all of your options, converting your 401(k) assets to Roth 401(k) assets should be carefully examined, especially with the assistance of a tax professional, to make sure it is a good choice for your particular situation.

Rule of thumb: If you have maxed out contributions to your employer-sponsored plans and still want to save more for retirement, or maybe your employer doesn't offer a retirement plan, you may want to consider other retirement savings vehicles.

4. Use Roth IRA accounts.

Roth accounts are a great retirement-savings tool if they are used in the right way. Anyone younger than age fifty-five should consider funding Roth IRA accounts instead of, or possibly in addition to, other retirement savings vehicles.

If you are older than age fifty-five, you may not have enough time to fully benefit from the tax-free withdrawal feature of Roth accounts compared to the tax-deferred compounding available in regular IRA accounts. Keep in mind that there are limitations on how much you can earn in order to qualify to open a Roth IRA account.

5. Consider funding an IRA account for yourself and a non-working spouse.

If your spouse does not work outside the home, you may want to consider funding an IRA account for him or her as an additional retirement savings vehicle for your family. However, these types of accounts should be considered after you have fully funded your employer-sponsored retirement plan and your own IRA or Roth accounts.

If your spouse is working, he or she may have access to retirement plans through his or her employer, and these should be fully funded, if possible.

6. Pay attention to your retirement investments and asset allocation.

A common mistake made by too many people is to be too conservative in their retirement investments. If you have ten or more years until your planned retirement age, you should consider at least a moderate asset allocation.

How Much Is a "Moderate Allocation"?

Typically, this means a 60 to 70 percent allocation to growth investments such as stocks, commodities, and real estate, and 30 to 40 percent in income-oriented investments such as bonds and money market funds. Be sure that this allocation is reviewed regularly or rebalanced for you with an automatic rebalancing feature available with some retirement accounts.

7. Consider Roth IRA conversions from regular IRA accounts.

Converting a regular IRA account to a Roth IRA account can make a lot of sense *if you have adequate available cash to pay the income tax on the conversion* and are young enough to have time to recover from the hefty tax cost of the conversion.

If you are age fifty-five or younger, you are probably young enough to fully benefit from the conversion. Roth IRA conversions may not be right for everyone, but if your circumstances make it a good fit for you, it is a great thing, and you should consider it. Consult with your tax advisor as well as your financial advisor to determine if a Roth IRA conversion is right for you.

8. Watch deductibility rules on IRA accounts.

Your taxable income, your marital status, and the availability of an employer-sponsored retirement plan in which you could participate all affect whether or not you can deduct your contribution to your IRA account. Similar limitations exist for Roth IRA accounts. These income limitations for Roth IRA accounts do not apply to Roth 401(k) accounts.

9. Be strategic about withdrawals from retirement accounts.

When the time comes to begin withdrawing from retirement savings to meet your living expenses in retirement, think strategically about how and when to withdraw from tax-advantaged retirement accounts.

Rule of thumb: In general, it is best to capitalize on the tax-deferred status of retirement accounts by keeping the money in those accounts as long as possible. You are permitted to withdraw from regular IRA accounts and other retirement accounts after you turn fifty-nine and a half. However, you are not required to withdraw anything until you reach seventy and a half.

Between age fifty-nine and a half and seventy and a half, consider withdrawing at least a portion of your financial needs from regular savings and investment accounts. These personal accounts likely do not have an immediate income tax on every withdrawal, as with standard IRA and 401(k) accounts.

This can help you keep your taxable income lower and preserve the tax-deferred compounding interest of retirement accounts as long as possible.

10. If you are considering early retirement, you need to know about Rule 72(t).

Ordinarily, if you tap into an IRA or other retirement account before age fifty-nine and a half, you will pay both ordinary income taxes on the withdrawal plus a 10 percent penalty tax for early withdrawal.

Depending on the state in which you live, you may pay state income taxes as well. The combined state, federal, and penalty tax bite can sometimes approach nearly half of the amount withdrawn.

However, if you are younger than fifty-nine and a half, you can retire early and set up a "series of substantially equal payments" from your retirement account that meet the specifications of IRS Rule 72(t), and you can totally avoid the 10 percent early withdrawal penalty. You will still have to pay federal income tax and state income tax, if applicable.

Another possibility besides using Rule 72(t) is that if your money is in an employer-sponsored retirement plan account, check with your employer for the withdrawal rules on your particular plan.

Some plans allow withdrawals as early as age fifty-five (thus completely circumventing the 10 percent early withdrawal penalty) if withdrawals are made *directly* from the employer's plan.

However, keep in mind that if you were to rollover your employer's plan account to an IRA rollover account, then the IRA withdrawal rules supersede the employer's plan rules, and you will pay the 10 percent penalty tax if you are younger than fifty-nine and a half.

When it comes to the whole area of retirement savings, investments, withdrawal strategies, and taxes, keeping track of what is or is not allowed in a given situation can get very complicated very quickly. Be sure to consult with qualified financial professional as well as your tax advisor to help guide you to what is best for your individual situation.

CHAPTER 41

WHAT SHOULD I KNOW ABOUT
THE DEFAULT INVESTMENTS IN
MY 401(K) OR 403(B) PLAN?

As a result of the Pension Protection Act of 2006, companies can offer balanced mutual funds, as well as target and lifecycle funds, among their QDIAs—qualified default investment alternatives.

A qualified default investment alternative is used when an employee is enrolled in a 401(k) plan and for whatever reason, does not make an investment selection on their own. Balanced funds create an assortment of investments that are intended to fit the group of employees as a whole, while target or lifecycle funds contain specific mixtures of investments targeted to an investor's age or retirement date.

TARGET (OR LIFECYCLE) FUNDS

These both have become popular with many retirement plans as default investments and with many individual investors, as well. Why the demand? Well, in part, these types of funds have been positioned as "no-brainer" investments for those individuals without the time, inclination, or knowledge to choose investments for themselves.

What is also important to know about these default investments in 401(k) plans is that *employers are not liable for employees' money lost* while invested in a qualified default investment. However, the employer is responsible for doing the due diligence to select the investments, for monitoring the investments' performance, and for deciding whether to keep or let go of those investments.

So, does that mean that you can comfortably rely on default investments for your entire retirement investment strategy? No. It will almost always be better for you to consider your individual circumstances, your comfort level with various investments, and then tailor your investment strategy to suit you—not some generic version of you.

So, how should you evaluate a target-date, lifecycle, or other supposedly one-size-fits-all investment vehicle?

ASK SMART QUESTIONS. HERE ARE FOUR TO GET YOU STARTED:

Question #1: Do you know how much money you will need to retire comfortably?

This is one of the questions you should start with based on your age and your vision of what you really want in your retirement. It is one thing to invest in a fund that promises consistent growth until your retirement date, but what if you need more growth?

Or what if there are specific tax or spending issues that might interfere with putting the right amount of money into retirement investments each year? A mutual fund cannot ask you what your goals are or make sure you're investing enough.

It is important to ask the right questions and to seek out the right answers. For most people, it will be helpful to seek guidance from a qualified investment professional. A properly trained financial planner can help you ask the right questions and help you custom-tailor your investment strategy to suit your individual needs and goals.

Question #2: How did your employer select the funds you are being offered?

Obviously, employers want to make the right fund choices for their employees, but just because they are offering target funds does not mean they are offering the right target funds for you and your needs.

Keep in mind that most fund choices offered to companies for use in 401(k) plans are heavily marketed and might not necessarily be the lowest cost or most efficient investment choices available in the marketplace.

Wishing upon Morningstar...

One resource you can use is to check the Morningstar rating of any fund your 401(k) invests in. Morningstar is one of the leaders in supplying detailed information on investments that can be used to comparison shop for just the right investments that suit your needs. You can access Morningstar investment information online at www.morningstar.com A great deal of information is available for free, and for a small fee, even more information is available.

If you are consulting with a qualified investment professional for help on developing your investment strategy, they will likely have access to the full, much more detailed professional version of the Morningstar data available to help you make good decisions.

Question #3: What if you leave your job and take your 401(k) with you?

What happens to your target investment plan then? You can certainly roll over these assets into another tax-advantaged retirement plan, but what will happen to your annual retirement savings strategy at that point? Always ask the right questions and seek out the right answers. The chapters on taxes, 25 through 27, will help you. Then, make adjustments as necessary to keep your retirement savings plan on track.

Question #4: What are you paying for in a target fund?

Granted, the investment choices are being made for you in one of the pre-packaged investments, but what are you paying for those choices? Often, these funds are constructed based on a fund-of-funds structure that layers a fee on top of the fees incurred by the individual funds.

Always understand the fee structure of any fund you invest in. Excessive fees can cut into your net bottom-line return. For your 401(k) retirement plan investments, do not just rely on the employer's default investments.

Ask questions, do your own analysis, or seek help from a qualified investment professional to help you make smart decisions about your money. A trained financial expert such as a CERTIFIED FINANCIAL PLANNER™ professional can help you tailor your investment strategy to meet your specific goals in retirement that are not addressed by these one-size-fits-all plans.

CHAPTER 42

SHOULD I TAKE SOCIAL SECURITY BEFORE "NORMAL" RETIREMENT AGE?

There are always many questions about Social Security. It is a huge agency and sometimes consulting with a professional can help you cut through the fog of rules and regulations. One common question: Are you thinking about retiring early and possibly taking Social Security payments early? You certainly can do that, however, it may not be the best thing for you to do. The Social Security rules will allow you to begin receiving payments as early as age sixty-two, even though normal retirement age is now sixty-six for many people. So why not take the payments early if you can? Well, there are some important issues to consider before you decide to take these payments early.

It might pay to wait.

First, you will receive a significantly reduced benefit, and *this reduction will last for the balance of your lifetime.* This reduced payment might not matter if you have plenty of other retirement savings to make up the difference and still be able to live your life as you choose. If you are married and your spouse will be claiming spousal benefits instead of his or her own benefit, this is even more significant, since the spousal benefit will be reduced as well. It will also affect the amount that your surviving spouse will receive in the form of widow/widower benefits from Social Security.

Watch for a tax impact.

One issue that many people are not aware of is that until you reach normal retirement age as defined by Social Security, you are very limited on what you can earn without affecting your income tax situation. Once you reach your normal retirement age, current law allows you to earn whatever you can without impacting your Social Security and income taxes.

The point here is that if you plan to retire early and take Social Security early, it is pretty important that you have enough overall income to support your lifestyle without working to produce earned income.

Limits on earnings.

If you needed to or wanted to work some during those early retirement years between age sixty-two and age sixty-six, you will be limited on what you can earn if you have signed up for Social Security. If you are thinking about retiring early, consider trying to make it without taking Social Security early.

In this way, you will keep your options open and maintain maximum flexibility.

CHAPTER 43

HOW MUCH SHOULD I WITHDRAW
FROM MY RETIREMENT ACCOUNT?

We have covered some of the tax implications in talking about employer-sponsored retirement plans. But there are always questions, especially when it is necessary to take money from a retirement account.

When most people think about drawing an income from retirement accounts, they think in terms of an interest rate or rate of return from their investments. Most will say something to the effect that they want to "live off the interest" and not "touch the principal." They feel that they are being safe with their money and, of course, they want to stretch out the use of their money to make the money last as long as they do. There is nothing inherently wrong with these statements or this line of thinking.

However, another way of thinking about the same topic that can be very helpful is to think in terms of withdrawal rate, instead of interest rate. There is an important difference between the two concepts. If we talk and think in terms of withdrawal rate, we then put ourselves on more solid financial footing. In retirement, we need our income to grow over time to help keep up with inflation. If we invest our money in a well-balanced way, it is possible to grow the principal at a rate to keep up with inflation over time.

For example, when we advise our clients about retirement income, we generally recommend that they should plan to withdraw no more than 4 to 5 percent of principal in any given year. If they can get by on this 4 to 5 percent amount or even less, then we can have a reasonable degree of confidence that they can spend in this way for a very long time.

Our goal in setting up their withdrawal rate in this fashion is to preserve their purchasing power during their lifetime and preserve their lifetime savings for passing on to their heirs or making gifts to charity or whatever they choose. In other words, *by preserving their principal and limiting their spending, they are not likely to run out of money, no matter how long they live.* At the end of their lifetimes, they will still have an estate that can provide them an opportunity to make an important impact on the lives of their children or grandchildren or perhaps organizations that support causes they feel strongly about.

WHAT DOES "WITHDRAWAL RATE" MEAN TO ME?

Let's take a look as some examples of how we might use this 4 to 5 percent withdrawal rate concept in long-range retirement income planning. When someone asks, "How much should I save to be prepared for retirement?" I can calculate a simple estimate using the withdrawal rate concept. For example, at a 5 percent withdrawal rate, for every $10,000 of annual retirement income needed, you need $200,000 in retirement savings to support that $10,000 of annual income (5 percent of $200,000 = $10,000).

So, if you have a lifestyle that requires $50,000 of annual income, you will need to accumulate around $1 million in retirement savings to support that income level (5 percent of $1,000,000 = $50,000). This $1 million target does not take into consideration other sources of income, such as Social Security or retirement pensions.

THE COST OF OVERSPENDING.

But let's look at a different way to use this 4 to 5 percent withdrawal rate concept. Some time ago, I had a conversation with a couple who were referred to me for help. After listening to their story, it was clear that they had a problem with chronic overspending that seemed to be putting their long-term future at risk. They had about $1,500,000 in retirement savings, but they were spending at an annual rate of about $250,000 per year. At $250,000 per year, that is equivalent to almost a 17 percent spending rate. In today's investment environment, there are not many investments that can provide a 17 percent return. If they continued to spend at that rate, they could run out of money in just a few years. On the other hand, if they reigned in spending to 5 percent of principal or less, they would increase the chances of making their money last as long as they do.

You might be thinking, "How realistic is it that we could have investments that would support a 4 to 5 percent spending rate, adjusted for inflation, and then end up with a preservation of most or maybe all of the original principal?"

The answer is that it is fairly realistic. In fact, most charitable funds, university endowments, hospital endowments, and similar institutions have their money invested and make grants or other spending from the endowment funds at a rate of about 4 to 5 percent per year. Remember, these are institutions that expect to last long into the future, maybe even forever. With a well-managed investment portfolio and a 4 to 5 percent cap on spending, they are in a good position to achieve their long-term goals.

Now, as human beings, we won't last forever, but in retirement, we are at risk that we might just live a long time. We have to manage our financial affairs to stretch our money out to last as long as we do. One way we can do that is to plan to spend no more than 4 to 5 percent of whatever we have each year. This is the 4 to 5 percent withdrawal rate concept.

Remember to think in terms of withdrawal rate, not just interest rate or rate of return. This will keep you on a more solid footing as you plan your retirement years.

WHAT IS A "SAFE" WITHDRAWAL RATE FROM A RETIREMENT PLAN?

This is another way of asking the same kind of question. Many people ask me, "How much spendable income can I expect from my retirement savings?" Some will say, "I only want to spend the interest. I don't want to touch the principal. Can I do that and still have enough to meet my living expenses?"

Well, these are good questions and, in fact, both the questions and the answers have been the subject of many debates among investment professionals. The range of most of the professional discussions cites research to indicate that a "safe" withdrawal rate from a retirement account is probably between 4 and 6 percent of the principal each year. I have participated in some of these professional debates, and I have chosen to recommend to our clients to use a 4 to 5 percent withdrawal rate as a reasonable rate of withdrawal that will help preserve their principal.

I find other evidence of the soundness of this 4 to 5 percent withdrawal rate recommendation when I look at large endowment funds for schools, hospitals, and various charitable institutions. These endowment funds are supposed to be managed to support the endowment fund making gifts or grants each and every year, from now on. In other words, these funds are managed to produce a flow of money for making grants forever.

Forever is a very long time. Forever is longer than any of us will be in retirement and trying to live on our retirement savings. All of the endowments I have seen have a spending rate of around 5 percent per year. For retirement income planning purposes, the endowment's spending rate means the same thing as your retirement income withdrawal rate.

So, if you want to estimate what kind of income you can reasonably expect from your retirement savings, my suggestion is that you use 4 to 5 percent as an estimating factor. In other words, if you have $500,000 in retirement savings, you can reasonably expect to have about $25,000 in spendable income from your retirement savings each year at a 5 percent withdrawal rate. Plus, this withdrawal amount can be adjusted for inflation over time, assuming a portion of your money is invested to grow in value over time.

Notice that throughout this whole discussion, I have not used the terms "interest rate" or "rate of return." I have referred to withdrawal rate. The concept of withdrawal rate is an important concept to fully understand.

These pages on retirement are intended to help you transition smoothly into what for many is a very happy time of life. But let me step back a little and give you a parting gift from my files—my own notes about how to downsize for retirement.

CHAPTER 44

HOW SHOULD I DOWNSIZE AN EMPTY NEST?

As people move into their fifties and sixties, priorities sometimes change. The hours spent on home improvements and the sheer time necessary to maintain a full-sized home seem to be a little more of a burden. Not to mention that as kids move on and start their lives, there is all that unneeded space.

Another changing priority is that most Americans tend to turn on the gas in the last fifteen to twenty years of their working lives to make sure their retirement savings will be adequate to their needs. That is why the idea of downsizing is a good one to start early. It is also a good time for a financial check-up as well.

A trusted financial professional may not be able to help you sort out what dishes and furniture to sell or give away, but he or she would make a good first stop in developing a complete downsizing strategy involving assets, investments, career, and overall financial lifestyle planning.

DOWNSIZING CAN UPSIZE YOUR BOTTOM LINE.

With life expectancies lengthening, many people fifty to fifty-five years of age could conceivably be at only the midpoint of their lives. What is the chief advantage to downsizing? Handled correctly, it can save a lot of money. Selling a larger home—possibly one that still has a mortgage—in favor of a smaller house or condo that is completely paid off can save potentially tens of thousands of dollars in interest payments over time, while still building equity. The earlier the process starts, the better.

Here is a checklist of some considerations that may be helpful in downsizing your life:

Get advice first.

As mentioned, downsizing should be a holistic process—a chance for a check-up of your overall finances while identifying things, expenses, and habits in your life that you can comfortably jettison. It is helpful to set up a plan to extinguish debt in all of its forms and move on to a check-up of savings, investments, and estate matters. A trained financial professional can help guide you through this process.

Downsize potential health issues.

No matter what the final effect of health care reform, your out-of-pocket and premium-based health costs over time will be cheaper if you take steps to better maintain your health. Make weight and other personal health maintenance issues a new priority as you move into your preretirement years.

Plan for a retire-career.

You might be working for a company or organization that has a mandatory retirement age, or maybe you have a year in mind when it might finally be time to pack up and go. And while there is nothing wrong with a retirement devoted to travel and leisure activities, if you think you won't be able to afford to quit working completely, or if doing nothing will eventually drive you nuts, consider getting some career counseling/personality testing, and do some research now that will help you train for a new full- or part-time career for after you retire from your present job.

Start thinking about real estate and new places to live.

Today's retirees do not necessarily have to move to traditional retirement destinations. Telecommuting allows many people to continue their working lives and education from anywhere. For many people, the magic combination might involve cheaper real estate, desired weather and activities, travel options, and access to good doctors and quality health care facilities. Decide what kind of home you could see yourself living comfortably in at age seventy or eighty. This combination of factors might happen in a surprisingly large number of locations based on individual preference.

Talk to your family.

It is not only really important to discuss your expectations for later in life with your family members, but it is also important to get their feedback on what they consider good ideas for you. There may come a day when you need to rely on others for help, and it would be a good idea to identify how realistic that is. Also, if you are talking about downsizing certain assets or property that might have been in your family a long time, it is important to discuss that with others who might be affected by that decision.

Start weeding.

Physical downsizing is not something that is done in a month. Give yourself a year to go through each room in your home and prioritize what you are really going to need if you move to a smaller place. Make a list of what you hope to give to friends and family members and what you will donate or trash. Time will give you more opportunities to put good, usable items in the hands of people who could really use them. Develop a record-keeping system that fits you so you won't forget any decisions you have made along the way. Also, you might want to set up a separate area for family photos and other keepsakes that might have high emotional value.

Don't start upsizing later!

When you do move, chances are you will need to invest in some new household items or possibly furniture to match new surroundings. Try to avoid going overboard with this—thoughtful downsizing should prevent a lot of new spending for stuff you have already disposed of.

With a thoughtful downsizing process, you can simplify your life and save money in the process. Maybe it is worth considering. I hope the thought itself has been helpful—like the rest of this book.

AFTERWORD

It is my sincere hope that some portion of this book has resonated with you and prompted you to take positive action in some area of your life. As I said in the beginning, this book will likely best serve as a resource, to be referred to from time to time as needs present themselves in your life. I wish you the very best in planning and managing your personal financial affairs in such a way that you achieve complete peace of mind and ultimately make all of your life dreams come true.

ERIC HUTCHINSON, CFP®, AIF®, CHFC®, CLU®

With over thirty years of experience in the areas of financial planning, investments, estate-planning, and tax planning, Eric is a practicing financial planner, speaker, author, and frequent television guest. He has appeared on national television with Bloomberg in New York, and Little Rock, Arkansas television with the NBC, CBS, ABC, and FOX affiliates. He has been quoted in The New York Times, Consumer Reports, InvestmentNews, the Arkansas Democrat-Gazette, and many other publications. He has authored a number of booklets, articles, blogs, and was featured in the 2005 book, The Trusted Advisor. He is the author and producer of an innovative series of educational videos called "The Financial Briefing™." Professional affiliations include the Financial Planning Association, the CERTIFIED FINANCIAL PLANNER Board of Standards, and the Investment Management Consultants Association®. Eric is a graduate of the Arkansas State Chamber of Commerce Leadership Institute and has served on the St. Vincent Hospital Foundation Board and the Arkansas Community Foundation Board, where he serves as chairman of the finance committee. He is member of St. Peter's Episcopal Church in Conway, Arkansas, where he has served on the vestry, finance committee, and the board of the St. Peter's Endowment Fund. He also serves on the board of the Church Investment Group, an organization that provides money management services to Episcopal Churches and organizations across the United States. Eric lives in Conway, Arkansas, with his wife, Donna, where they enjoy travel, boating, and time with their grandchildren.

Printed in the USA
CPSIA information can be obtained
at www.ICGtesting.com
JSHW012050140824
68134JS00035B/3353